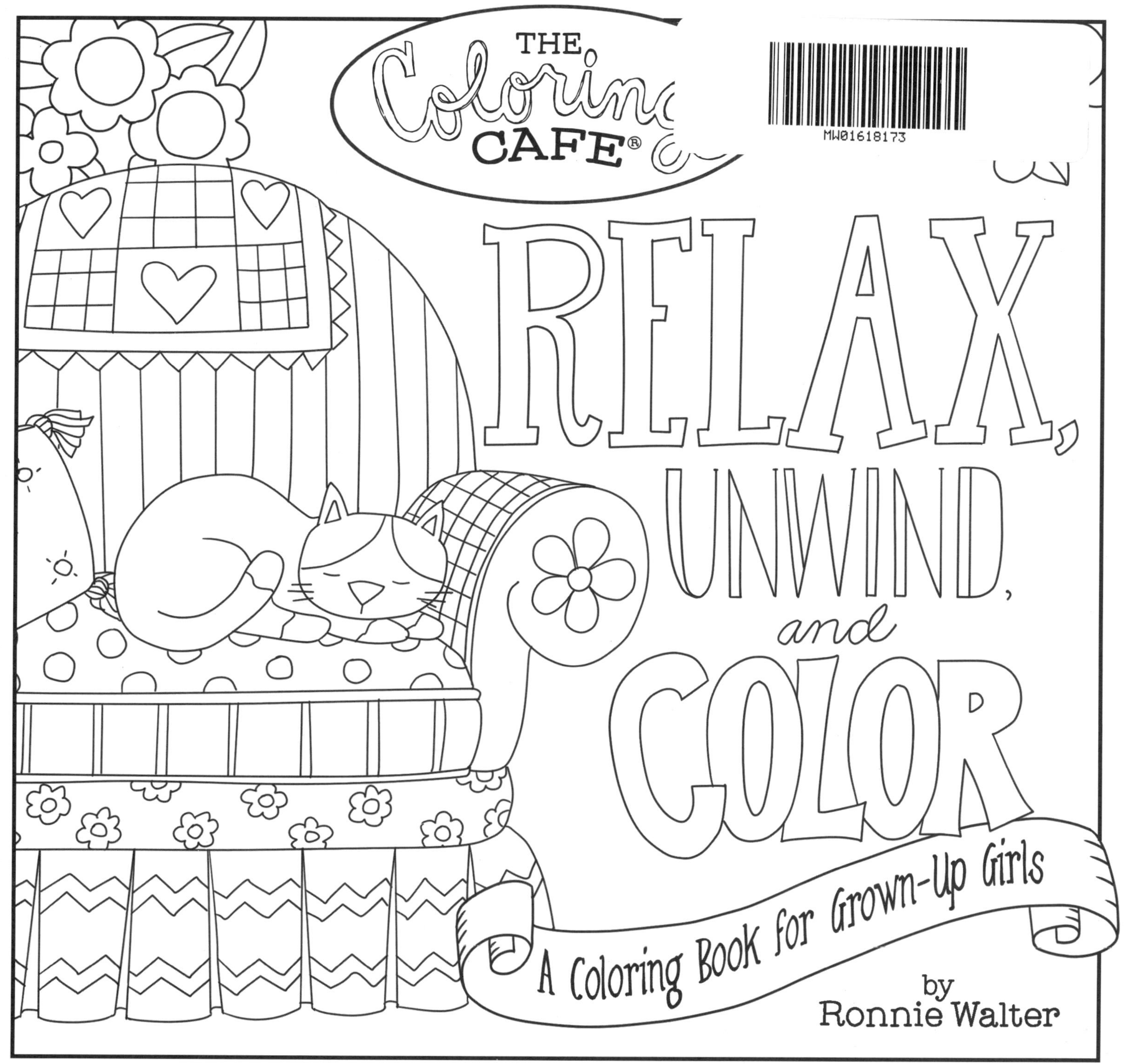
THE
Coloring
CAFE®
MW01618173
RELAX,
UNWIND,
and
COLOR
A Coloring Book for Grown-Up Girls
by
Ronnie Walter

ISBN-13: 978-1-56383-591-9
Item #2508

Printed in the USA
by G&R Publishing Co.

Distributed By:

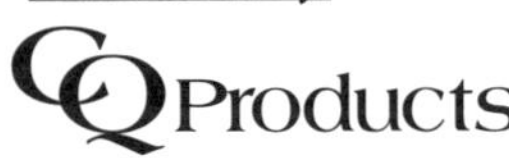

507 Industrial Street
Waverly, IA 50677

www.cqbookstore.com

gifts@cqbookstore.com

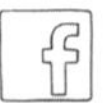 CQ Products

 CQ Products

 @cqproducts

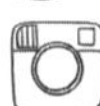 @cqproducts

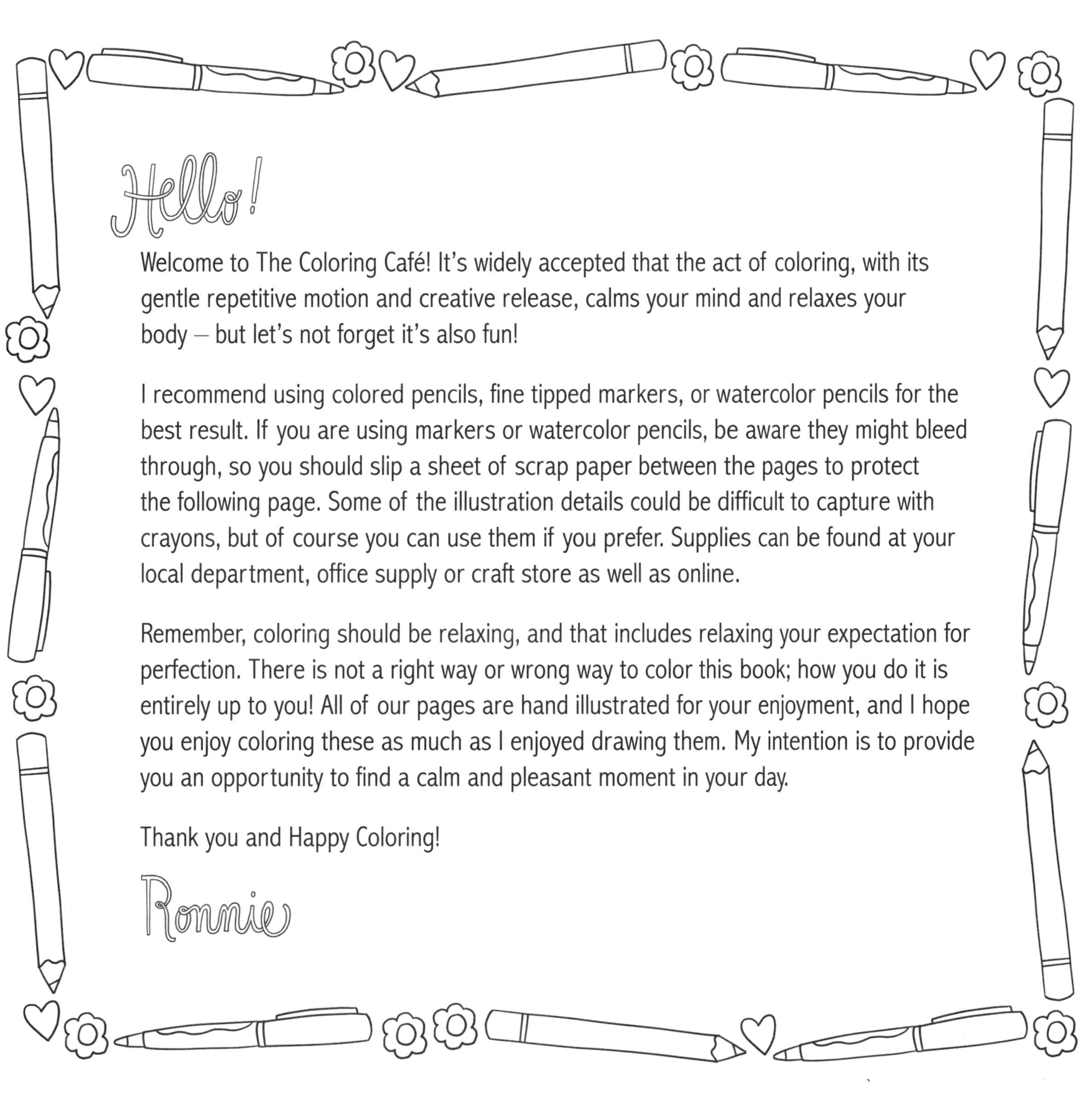

Hello!

Welcome to The Coloring Café! It's widely accepted that the act of coloring, with its gentle repetitive motion and creative release, calms your mind and relaxes your body – but let's not forget it's also fun!

I recommend using colored pencils, fine tipped markers, or watercolor pencils for the best result. If you are using markers or watercolor pencils, be aware they might bleed through, so you should slip a sheet of scrap paper between the pages to protect the following page. Some of the illustration details could be difficult to capture with crayons, but of course you can use them if you prefer. Supplies can be found at your local department, office supply or craft store as well as online.

Remember, coloring should be relaxing, and that includes relaxing your expectation for perfection. There is not a right way or wrong way to color this book; how you do it is entirely up to you! All of our pages are hand illustrated for your enjoyment, and I hope you enjoy coloring these as much as I enjoyed drawing them. My intention is to provide you an opportunity to find a calm and pleasant moment in your day.

Thank you and Happy Coloring!

Ronnie

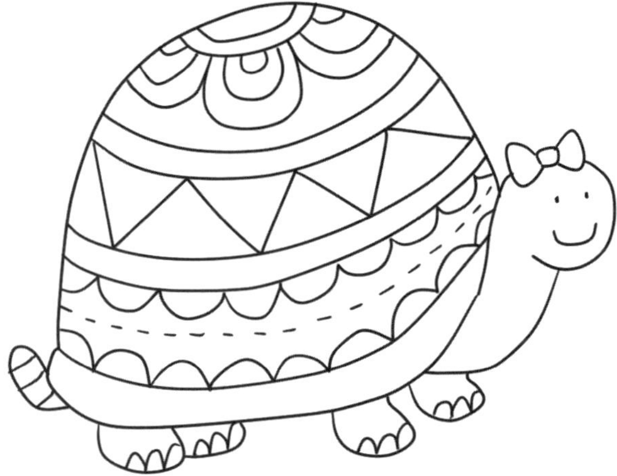

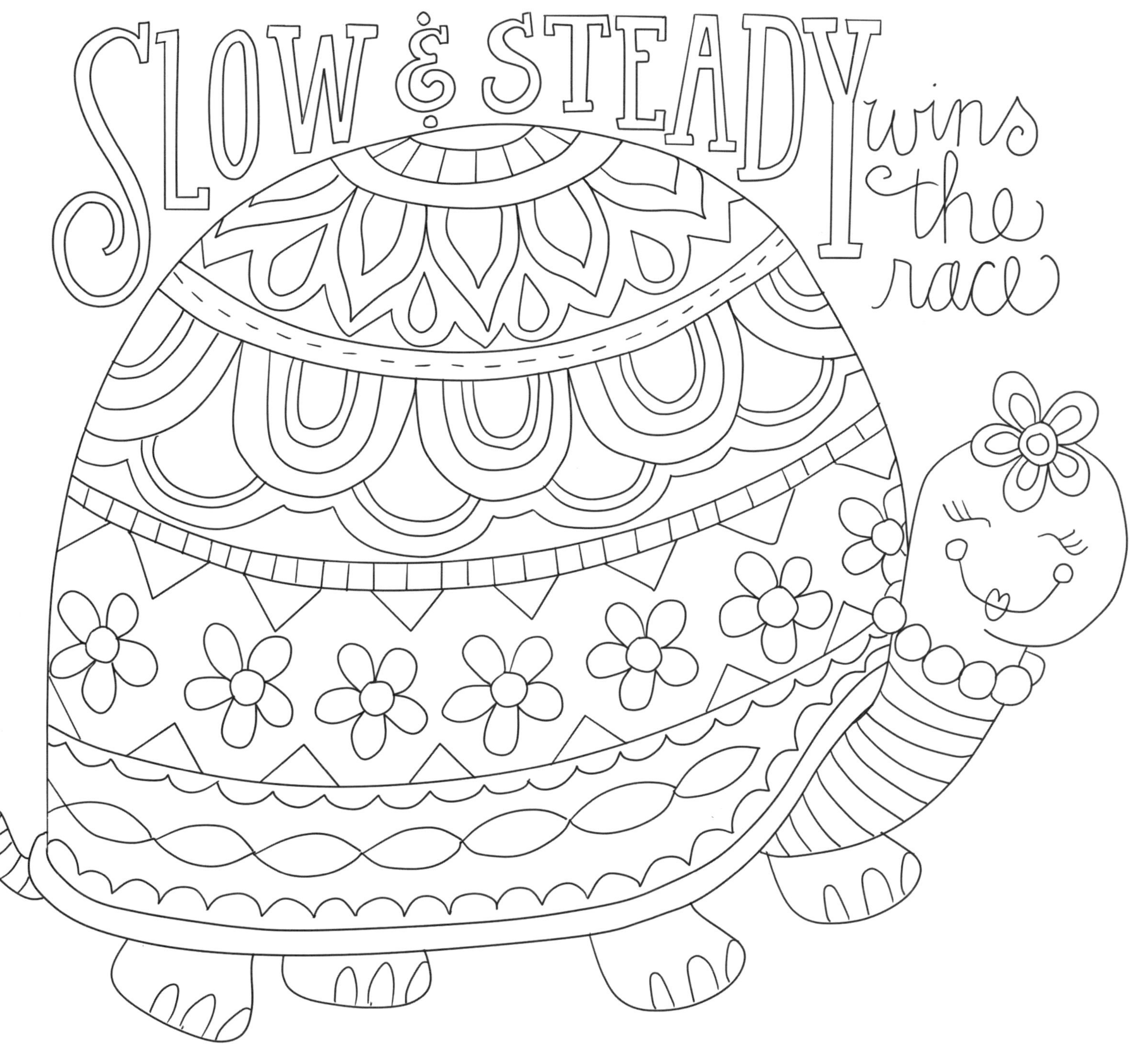
SLOW & STEADY
wins
the
race

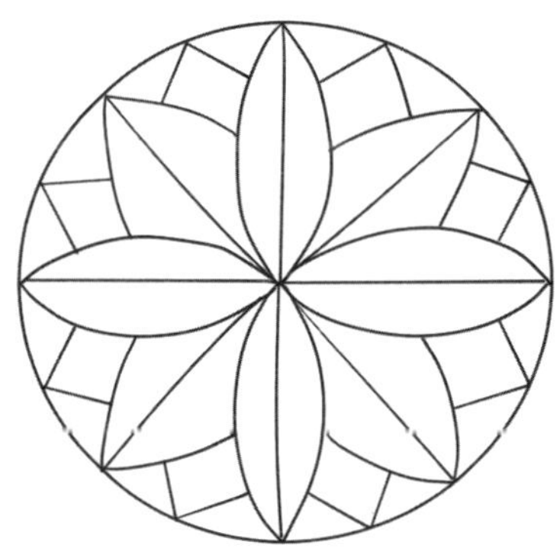

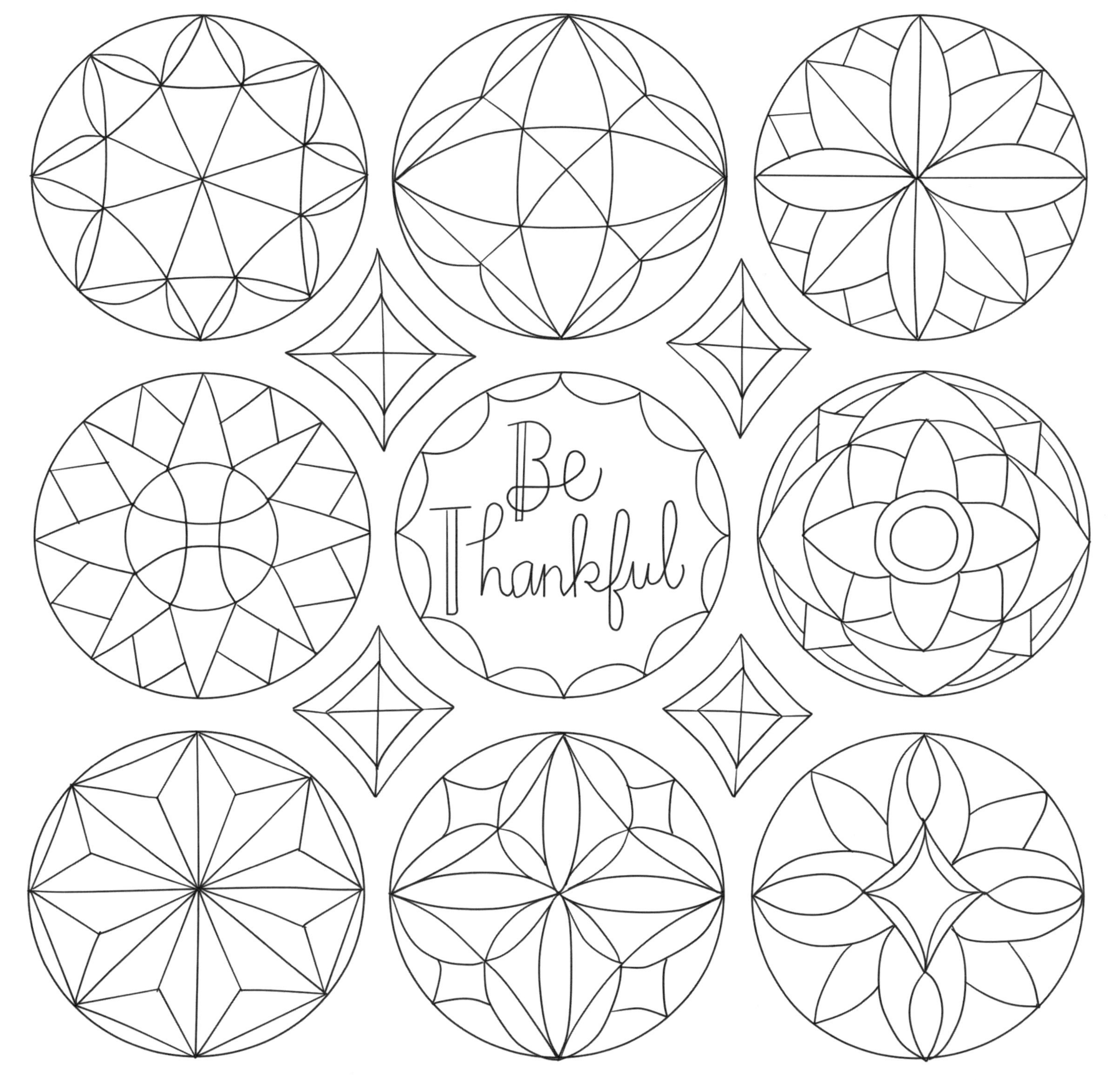
Be
Thankful

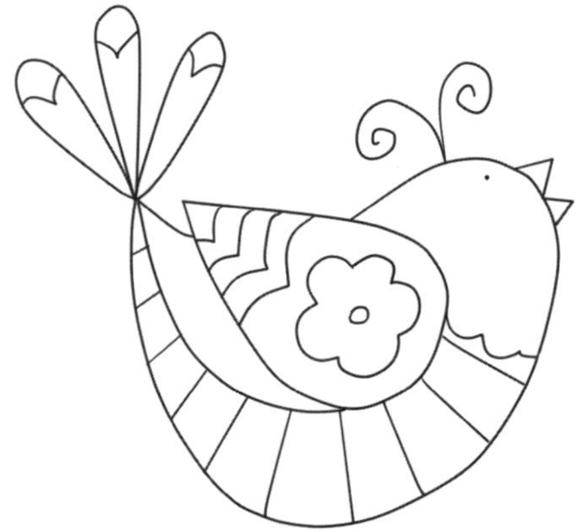

DREAM

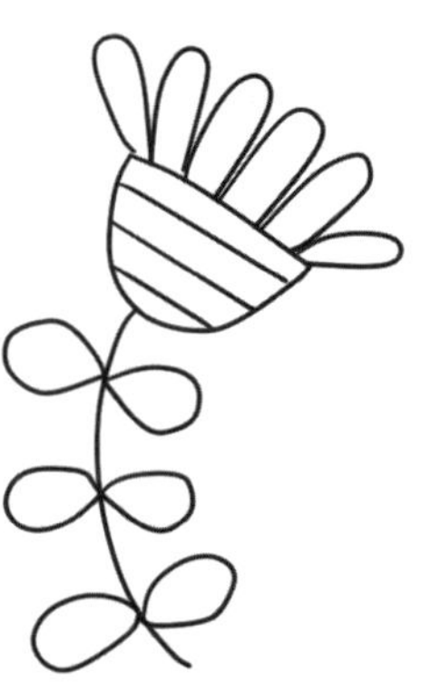

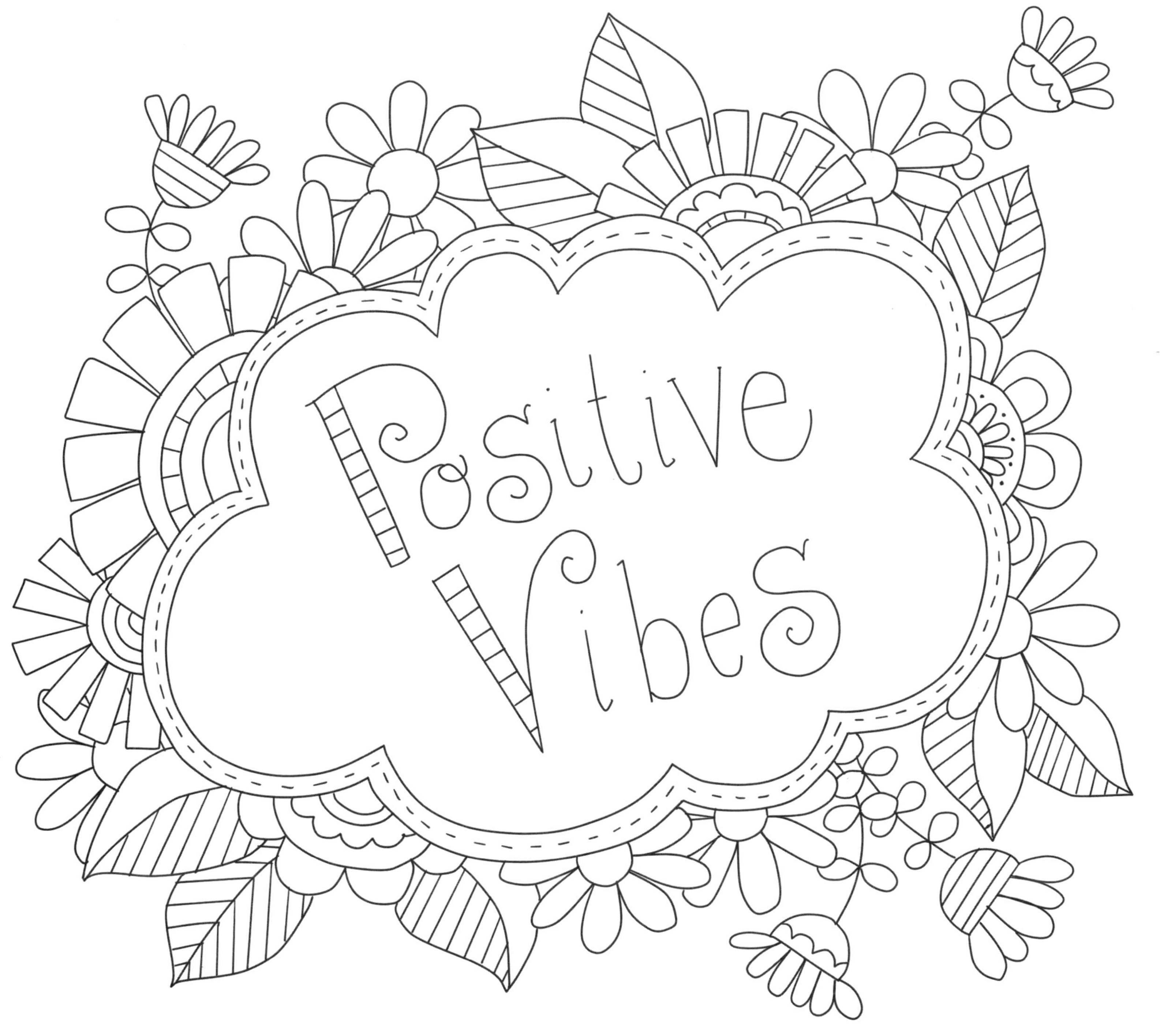
Positive Vibes

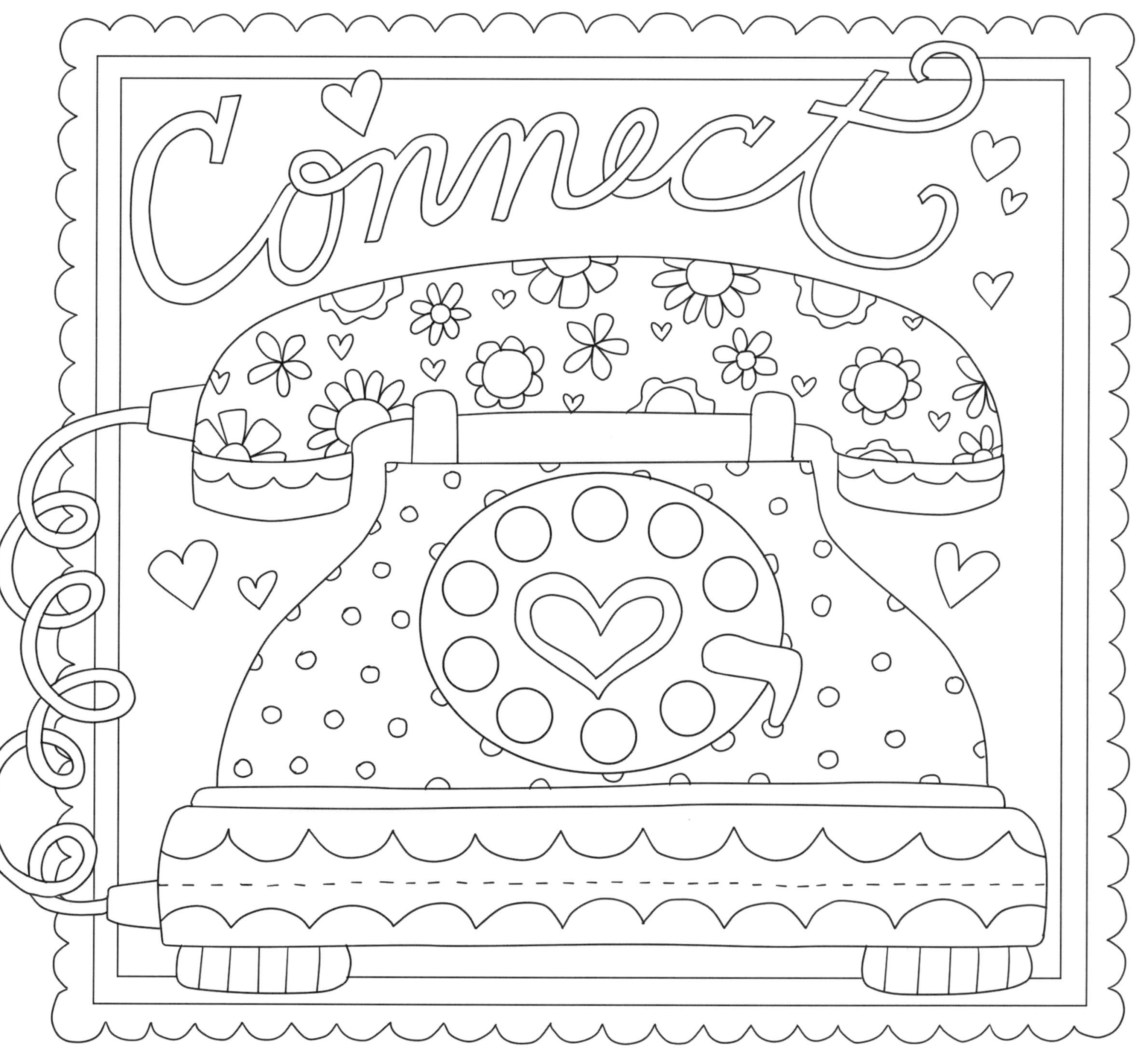
Connect

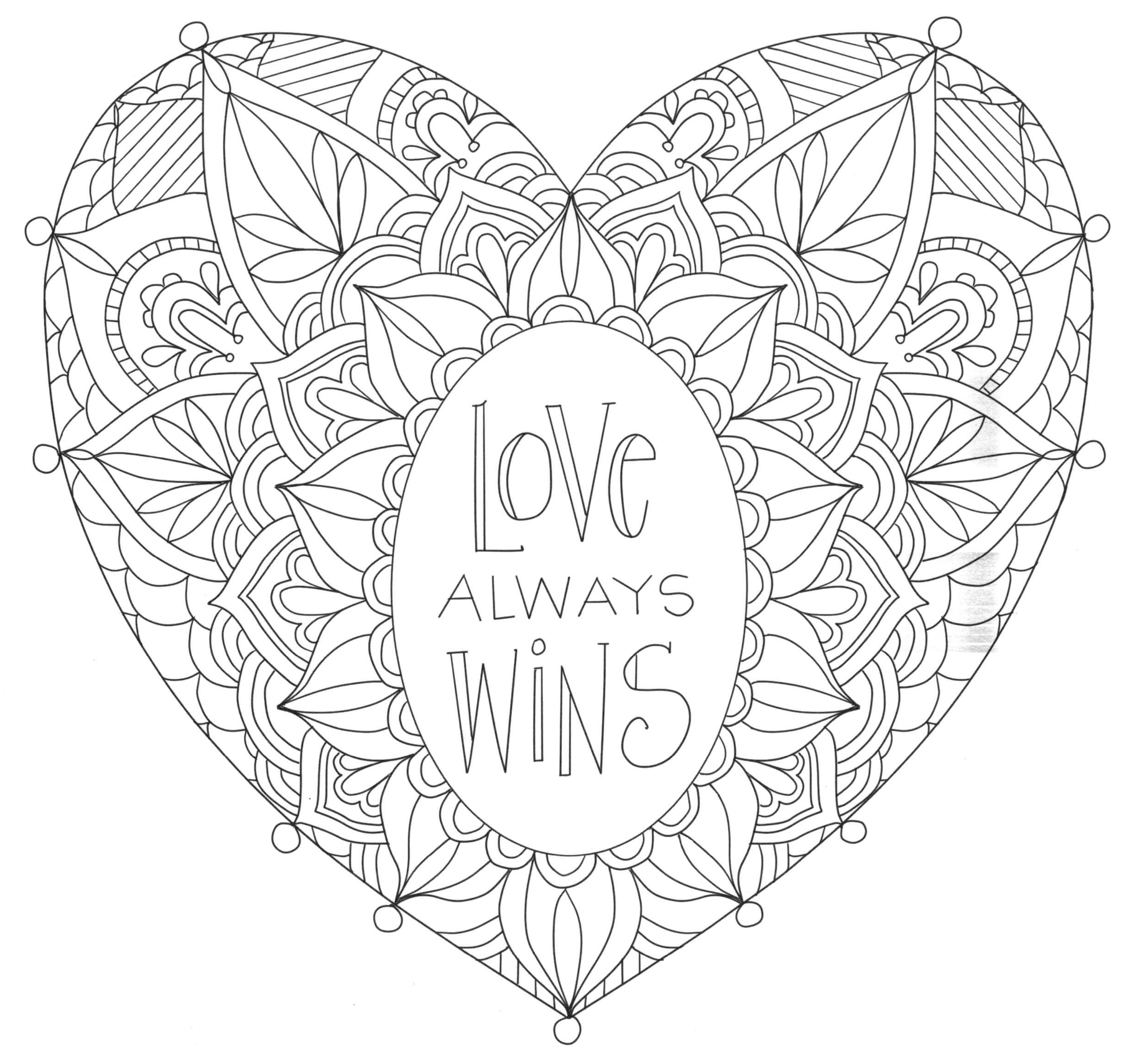
Love
ALWAYS
Wins

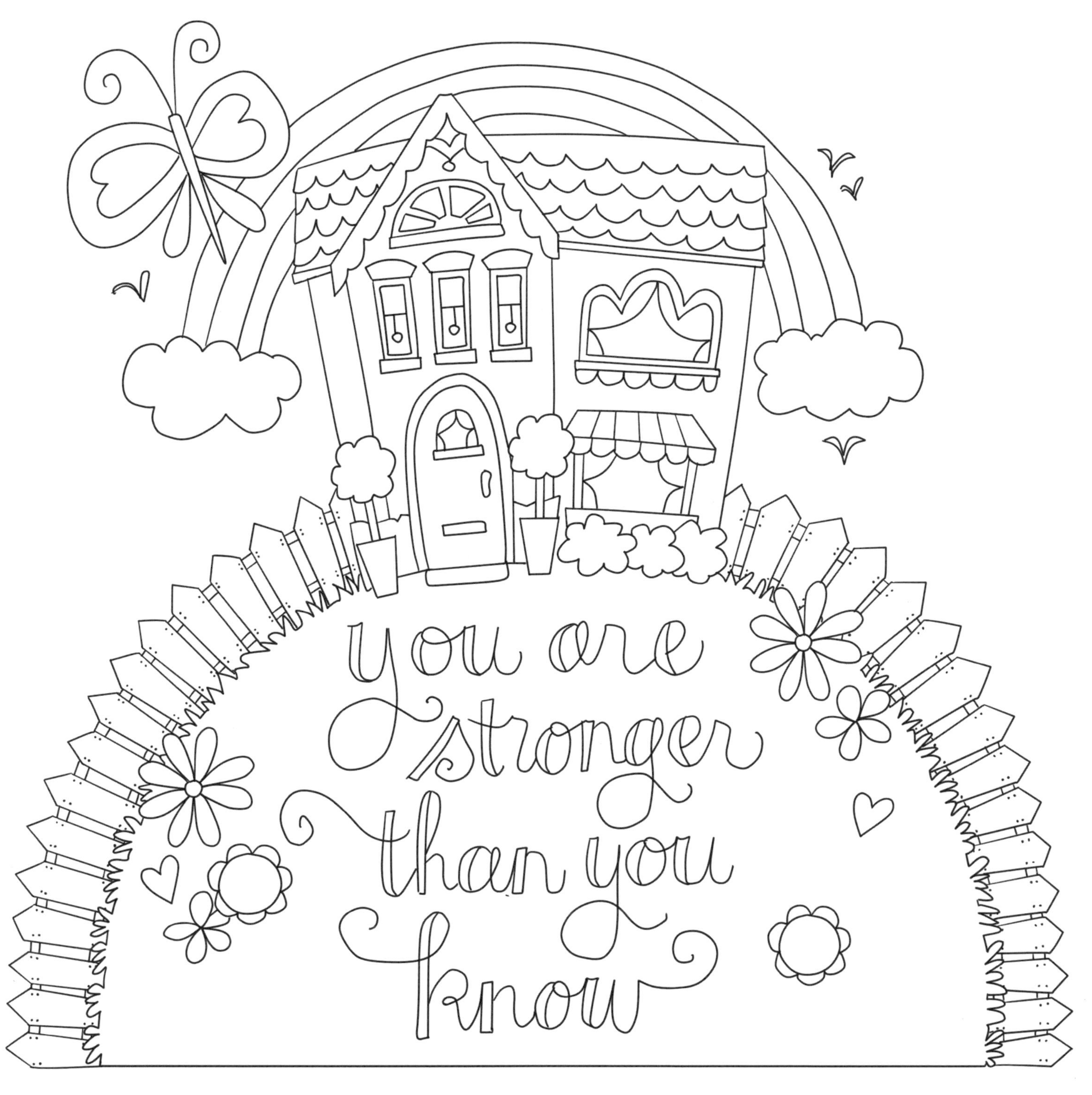
you are stronger than you know

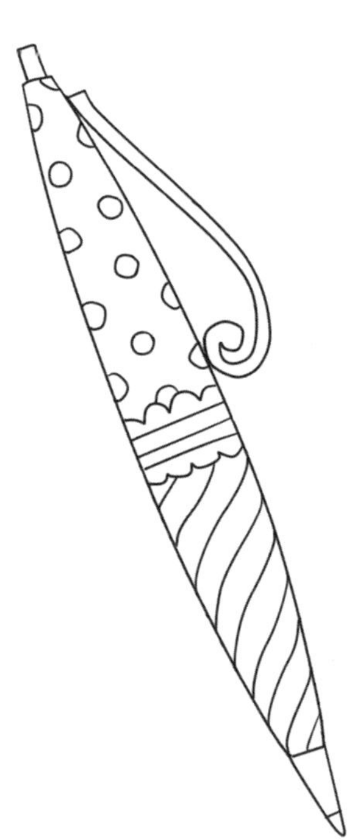

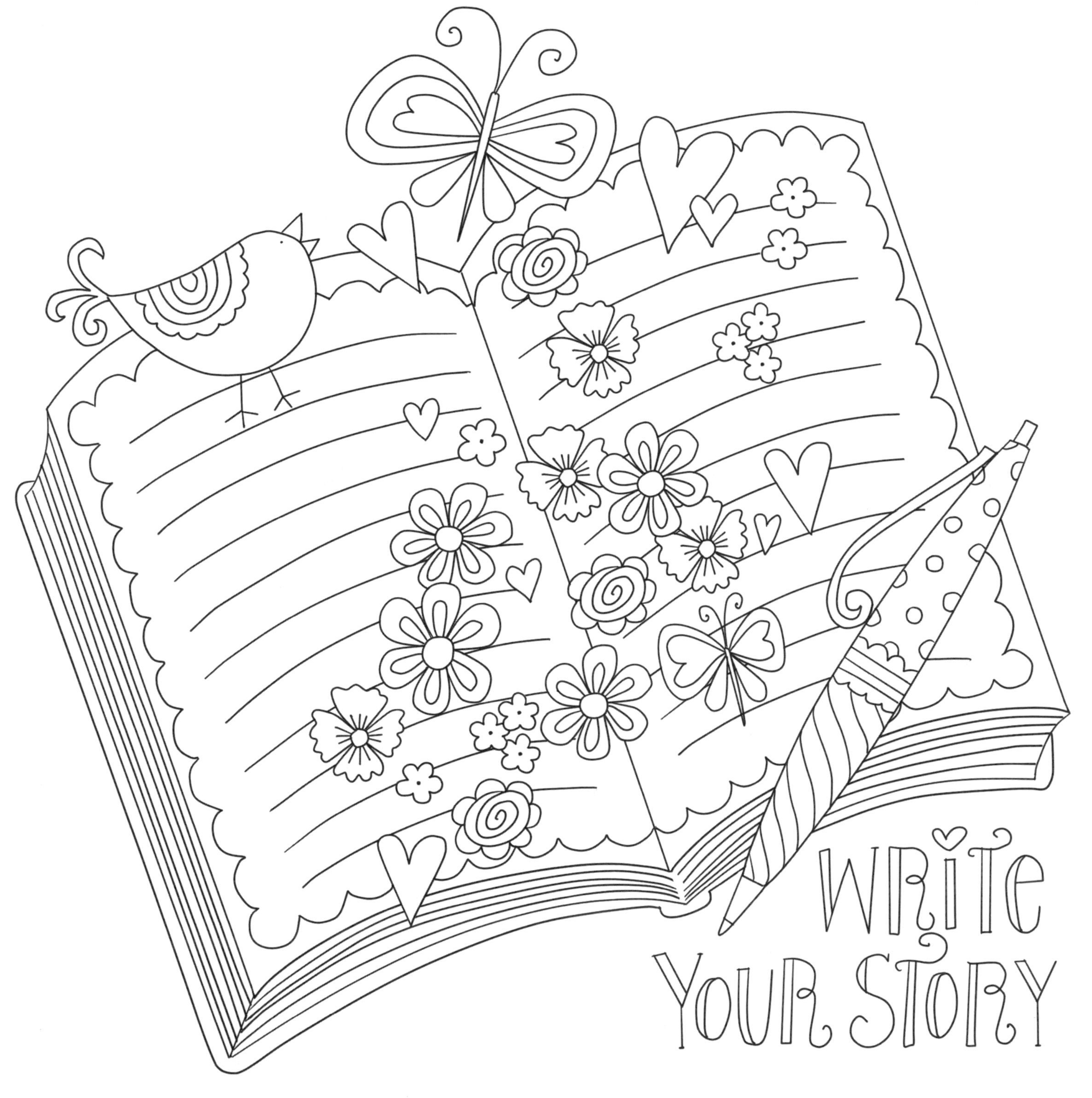
WRITE
YOUR STORY

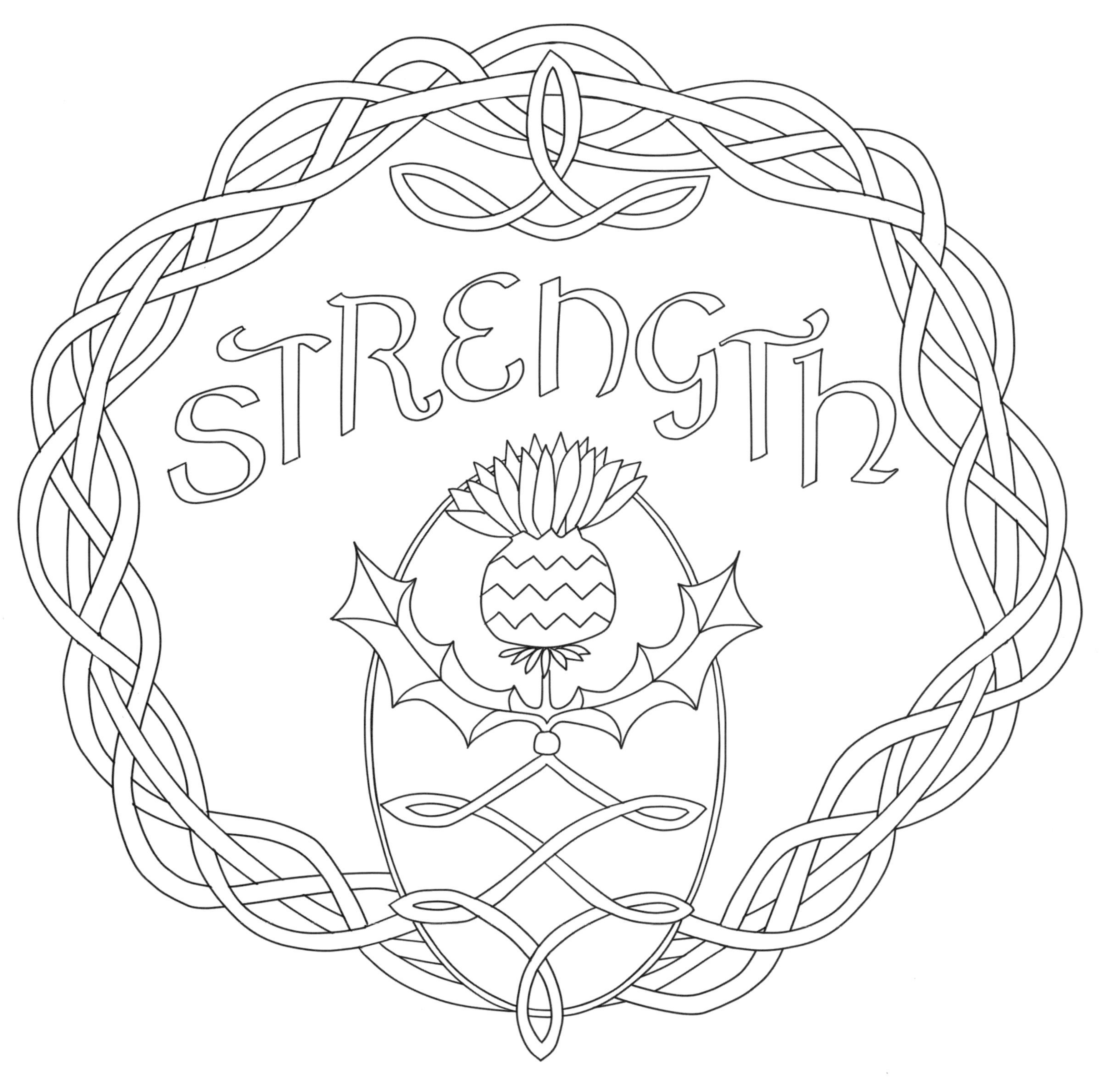
STRENGTH

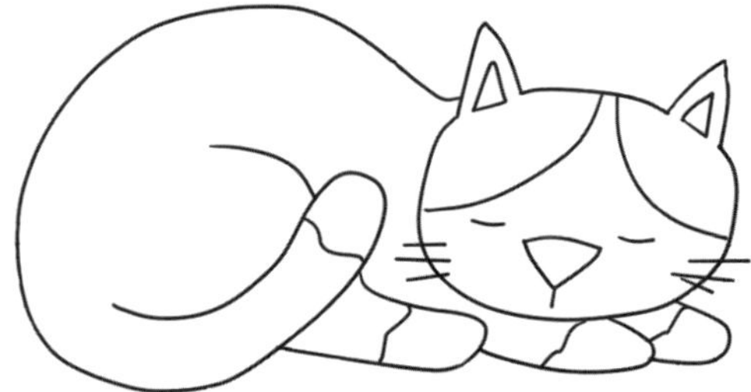

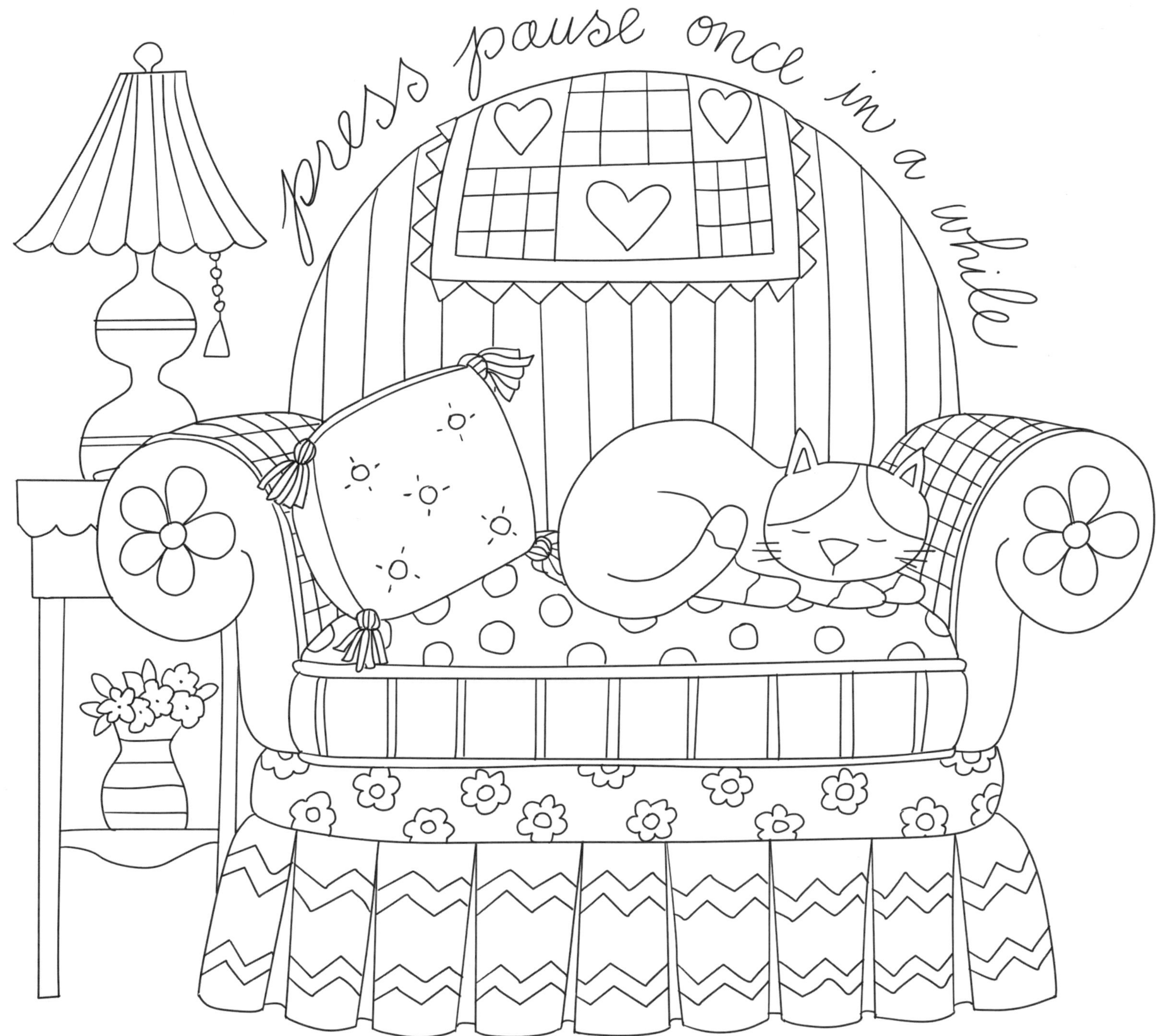
press pause once in a while

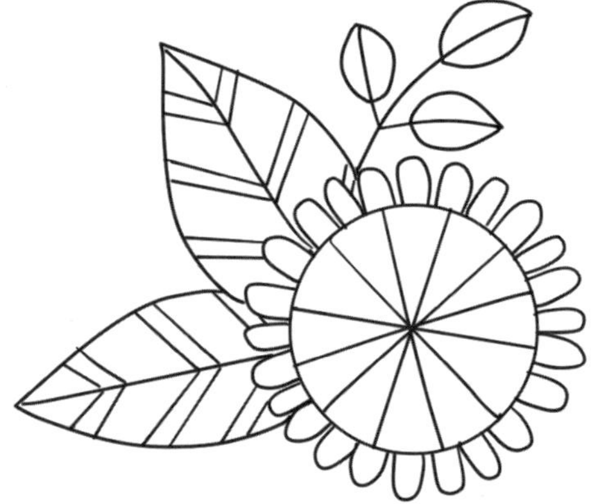

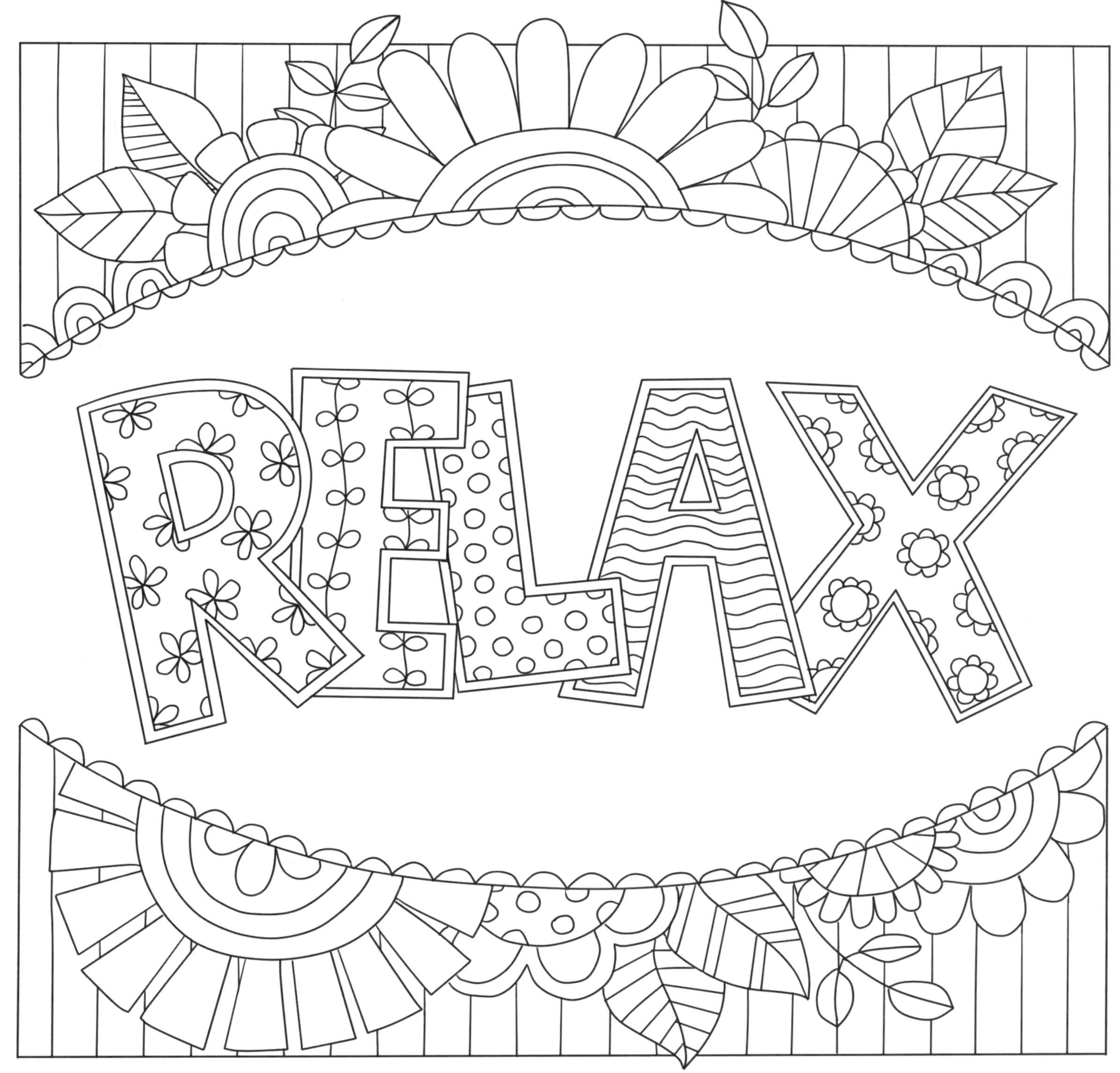
RELAX

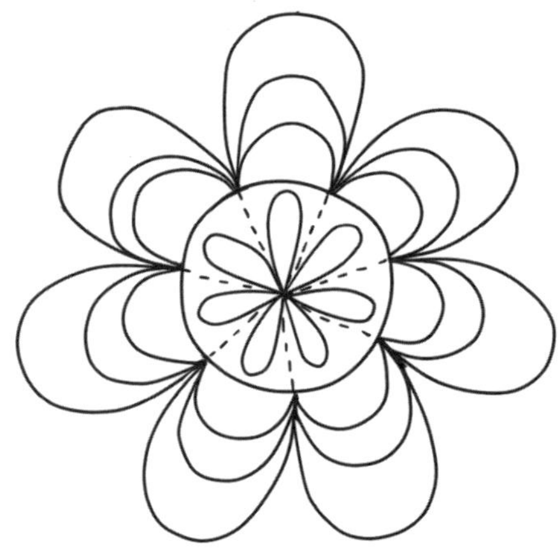

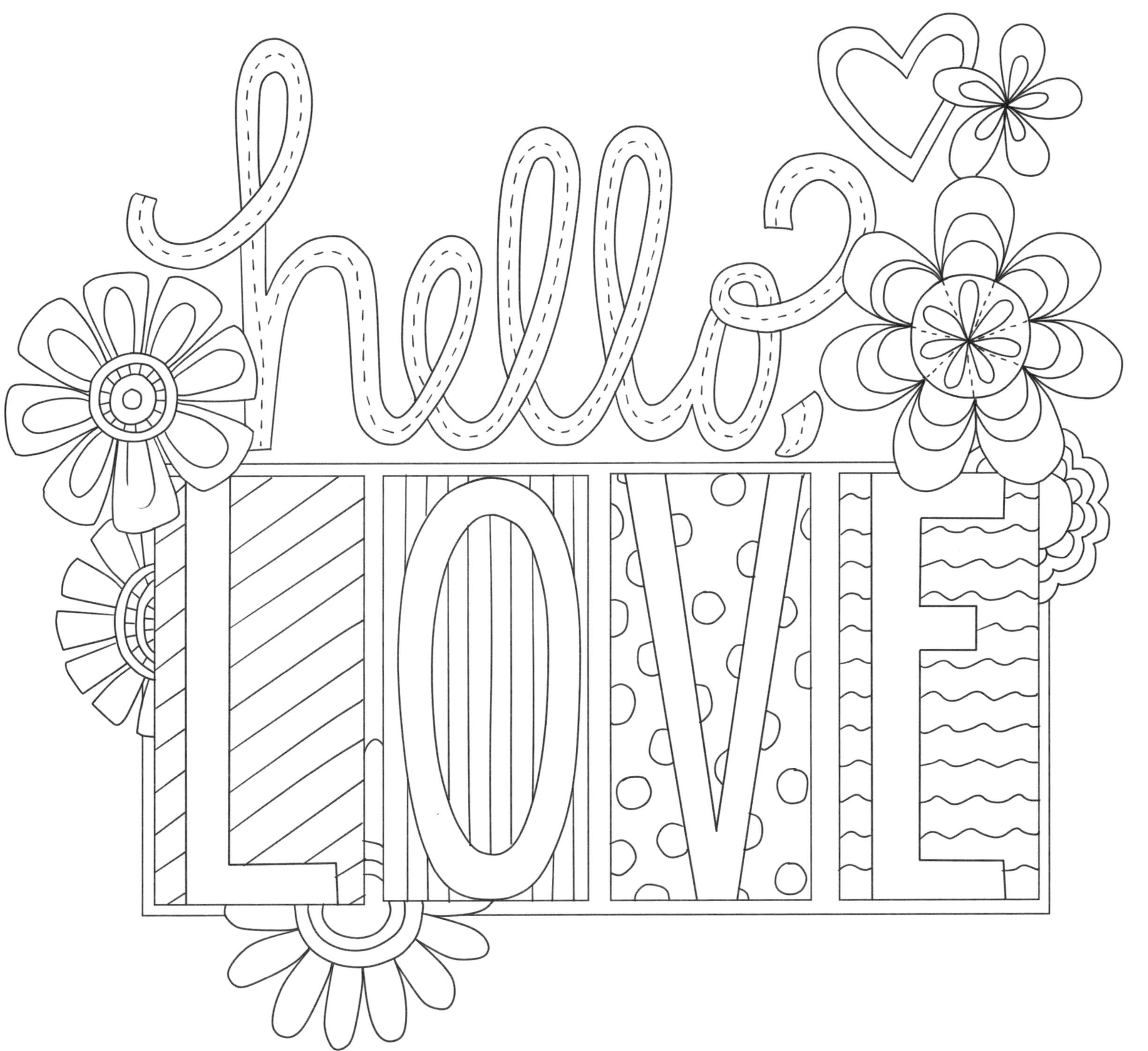
hello,
LOVE

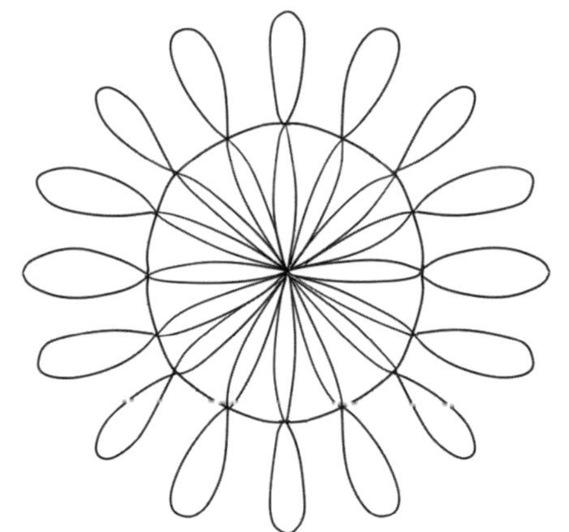

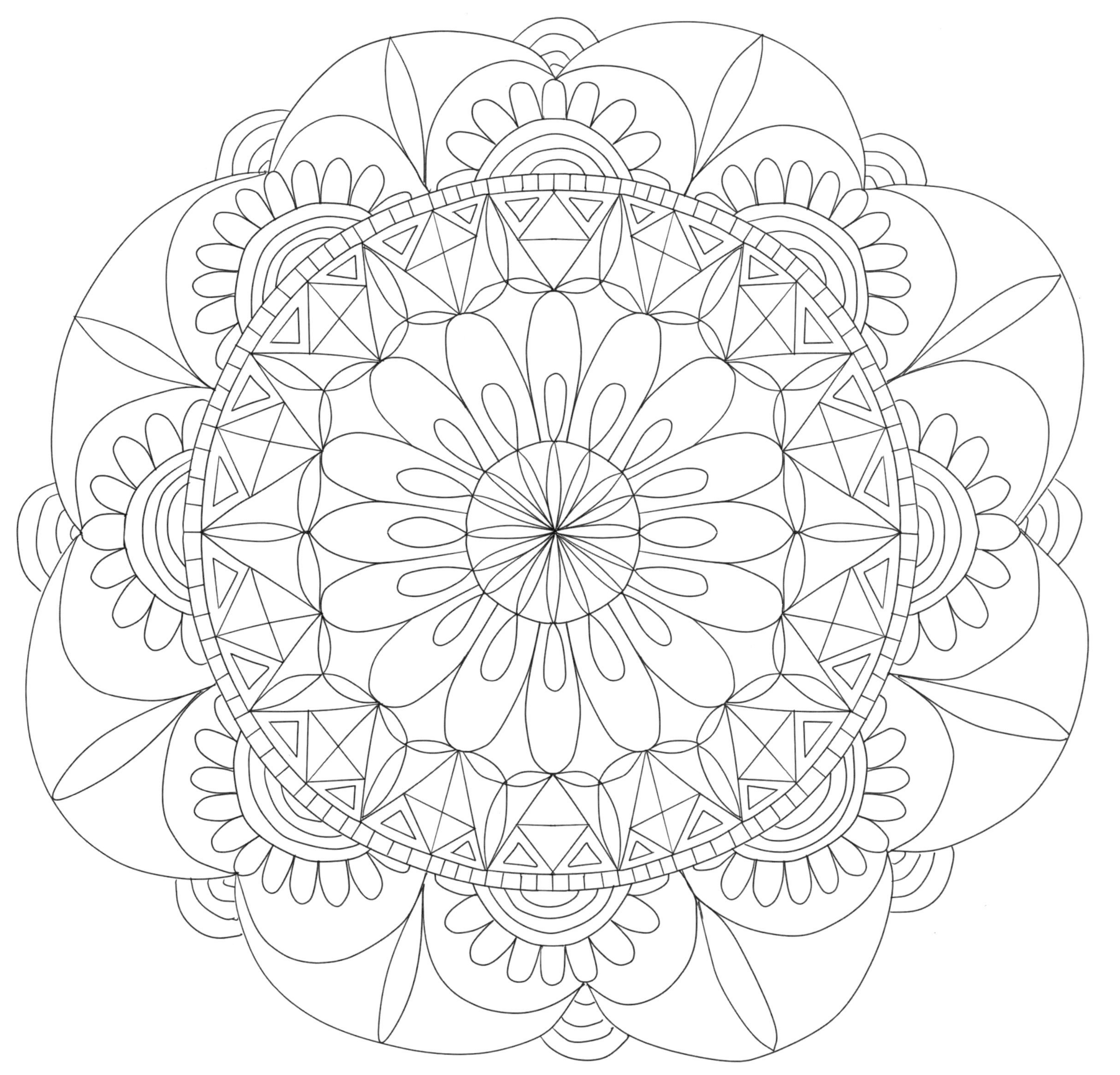

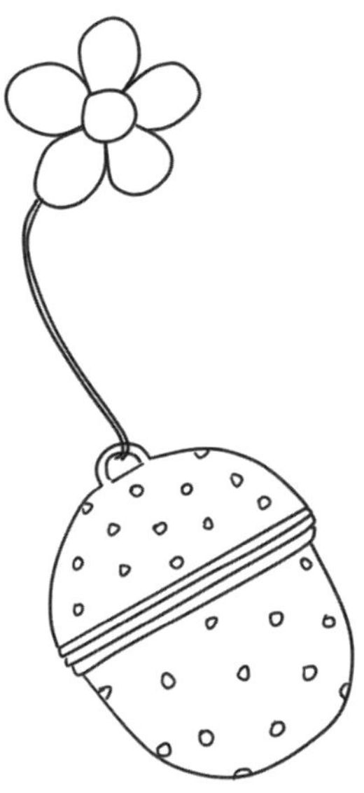

Tea is always a good idea

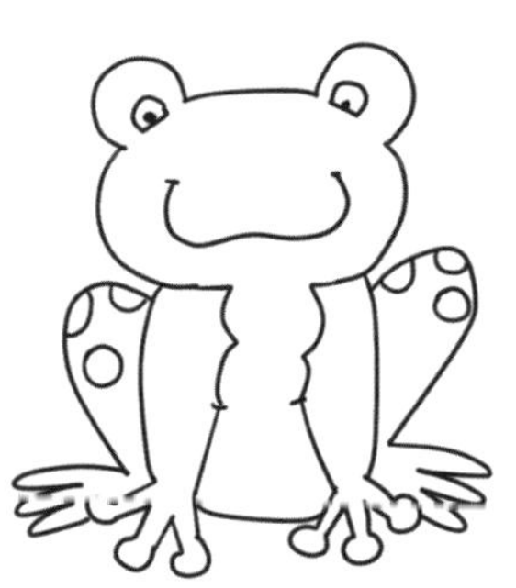

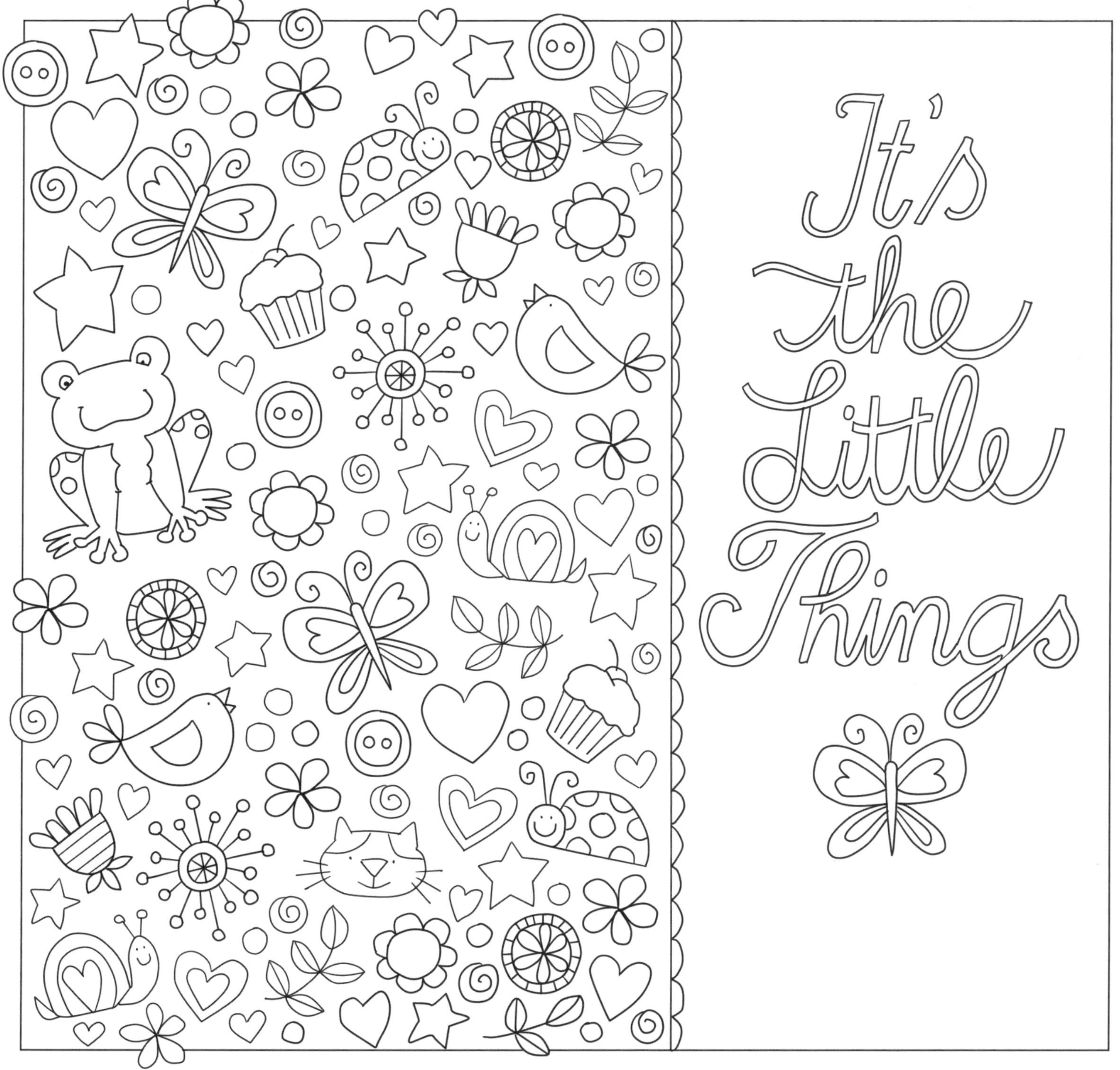
It's the Little Things

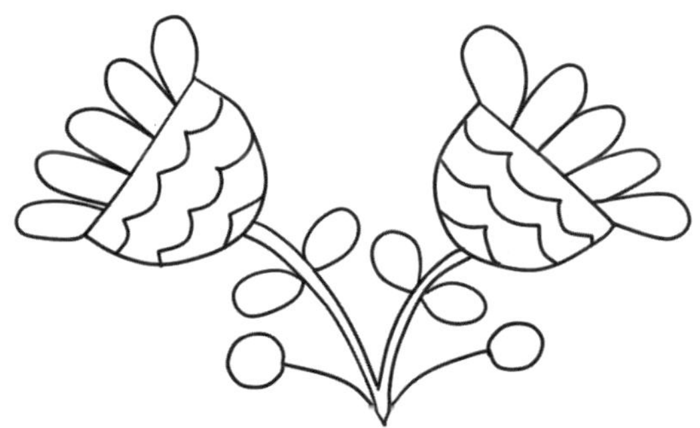

Let It Go

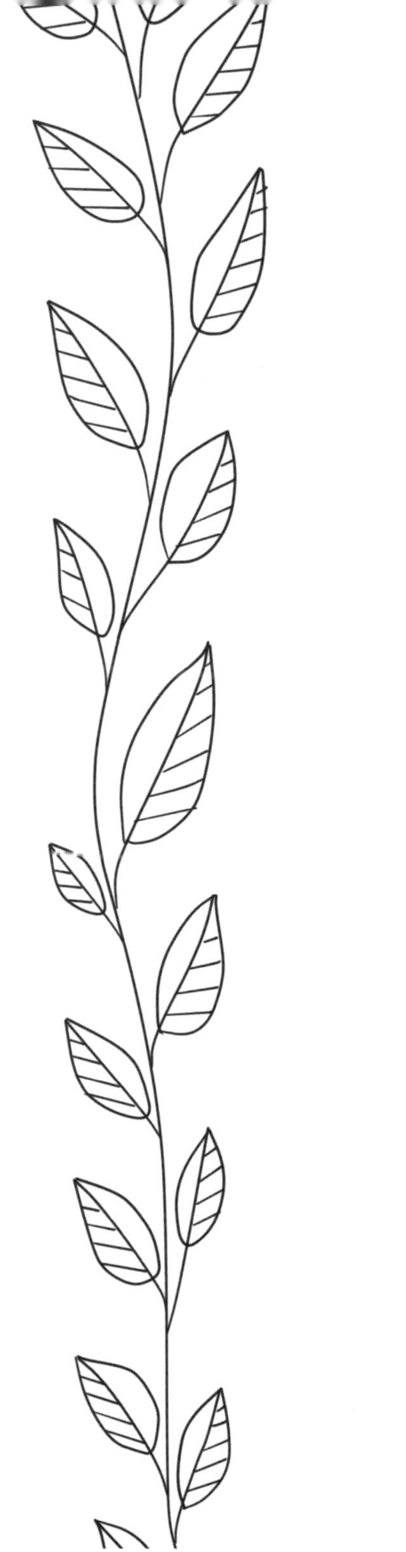

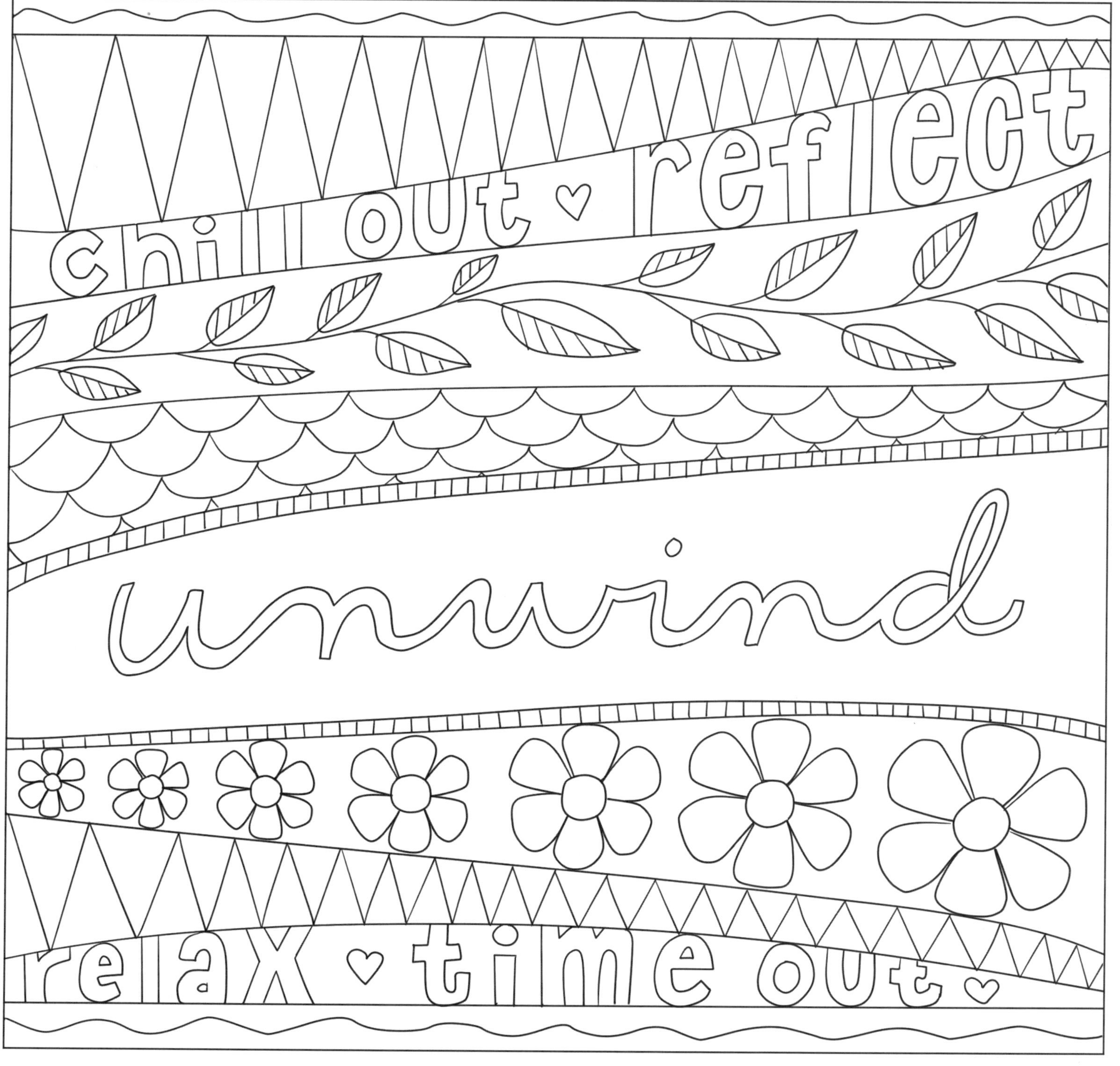
chill out ♡ reflect
unwind
relax ♡ time out ♡

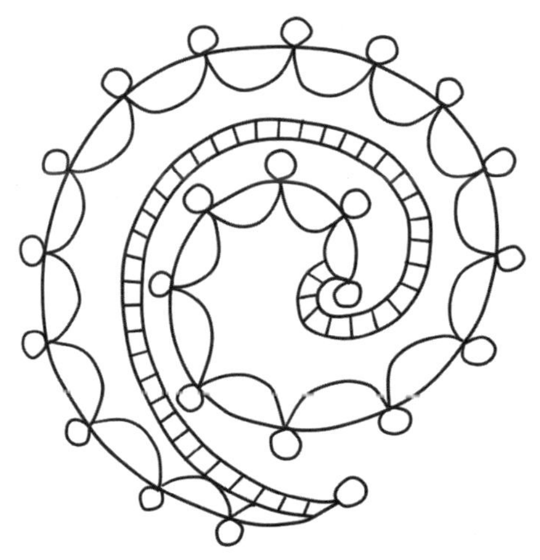

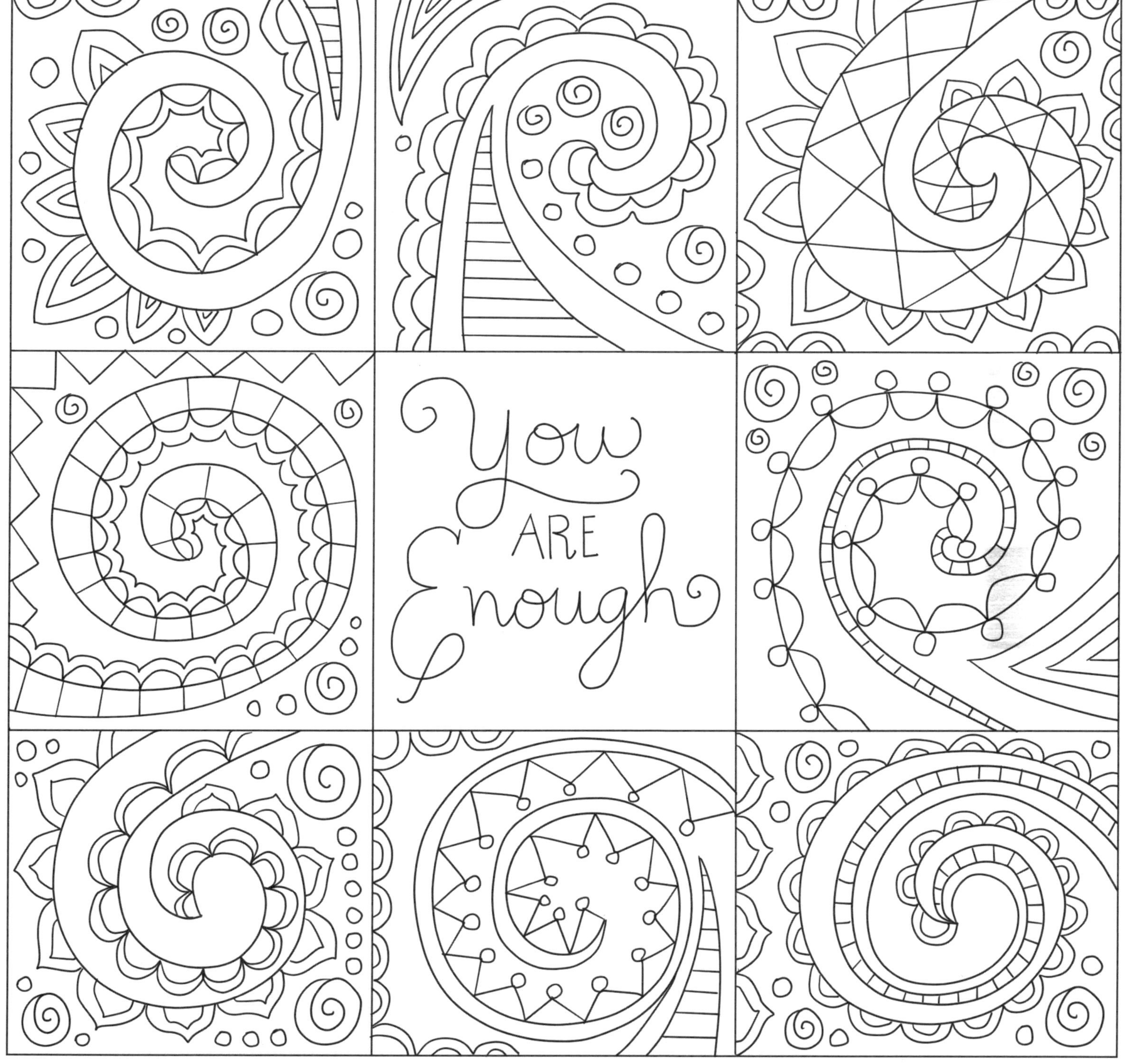
You
ARE
Enough

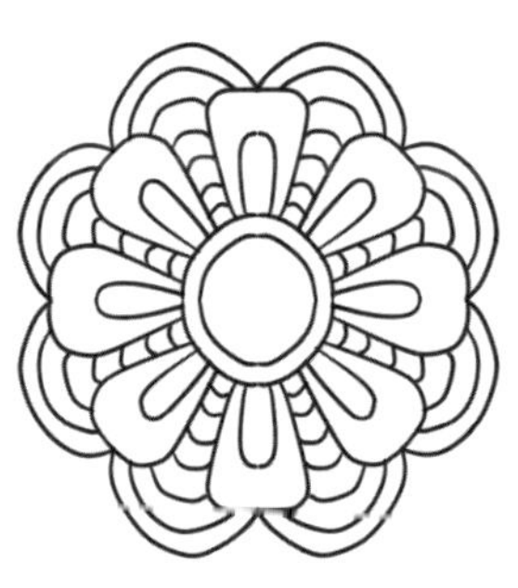

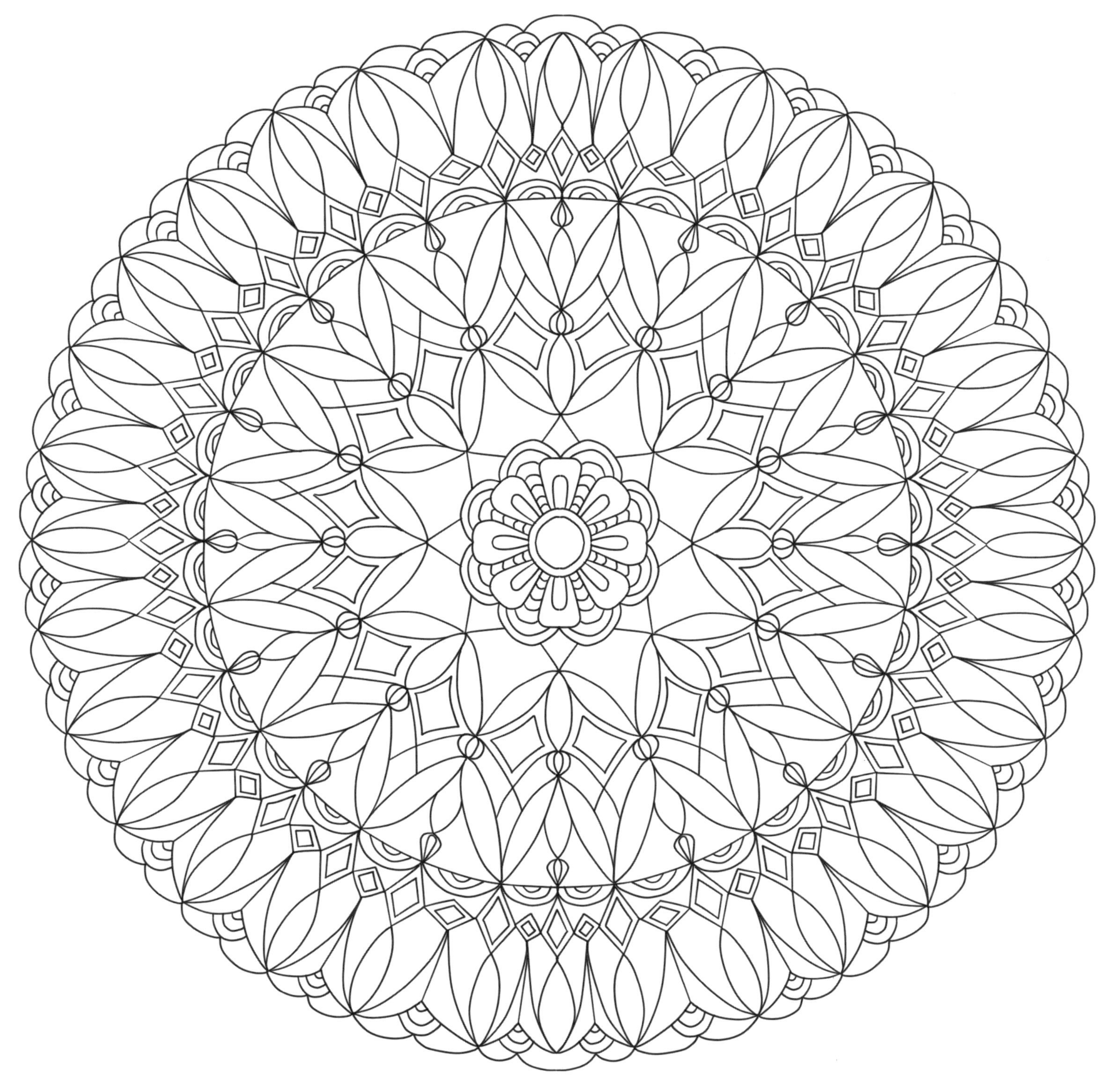

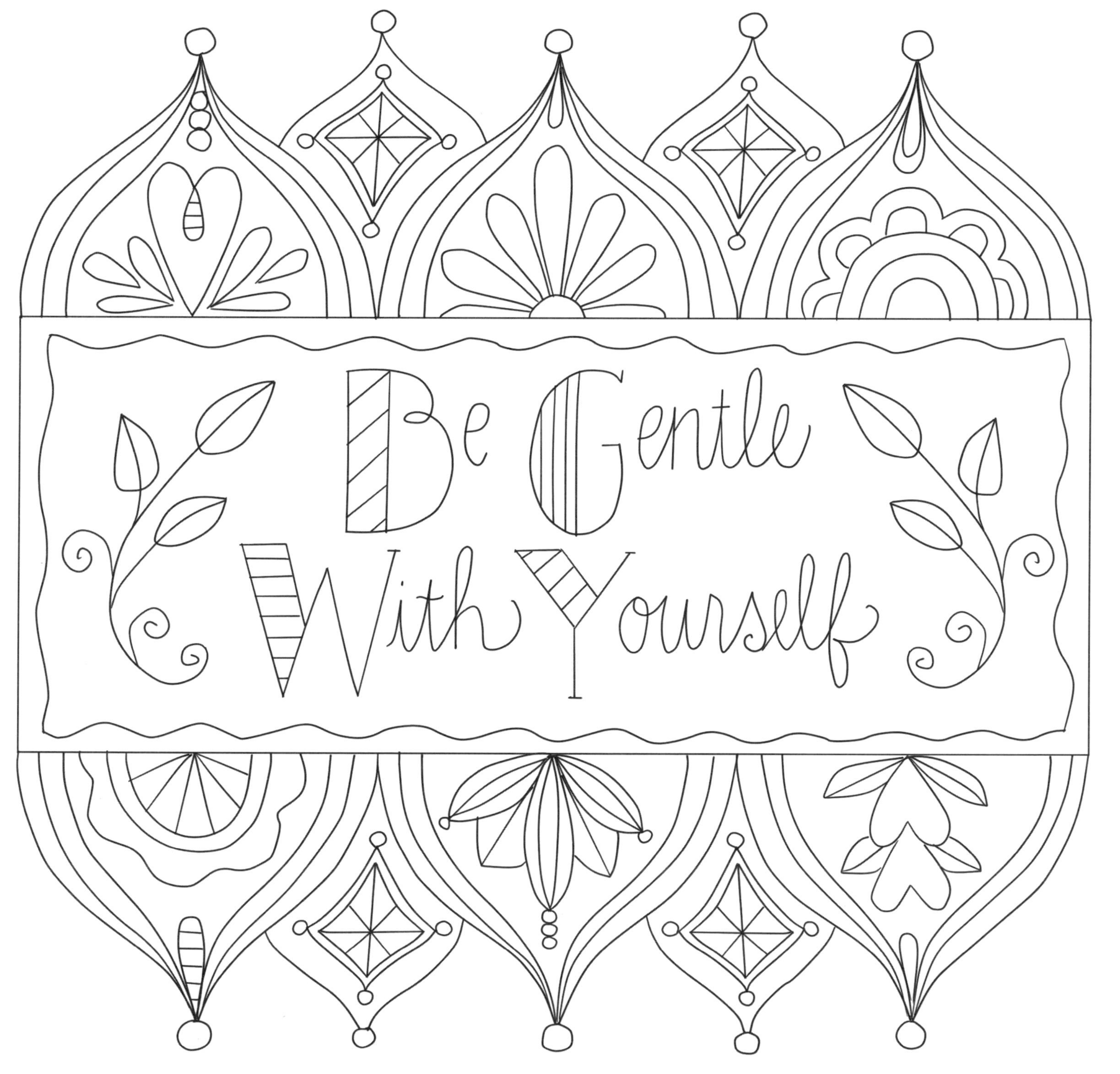
Be Gentle
With Yourself

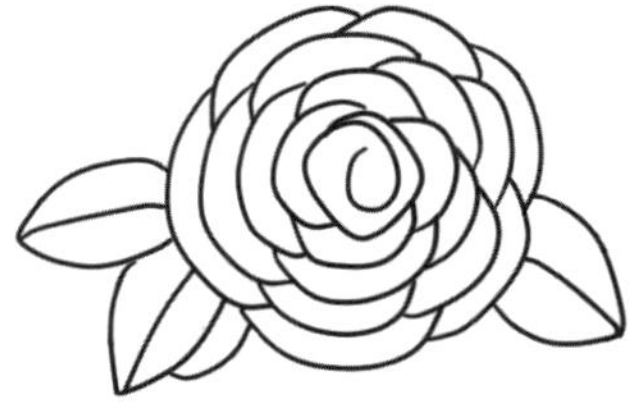

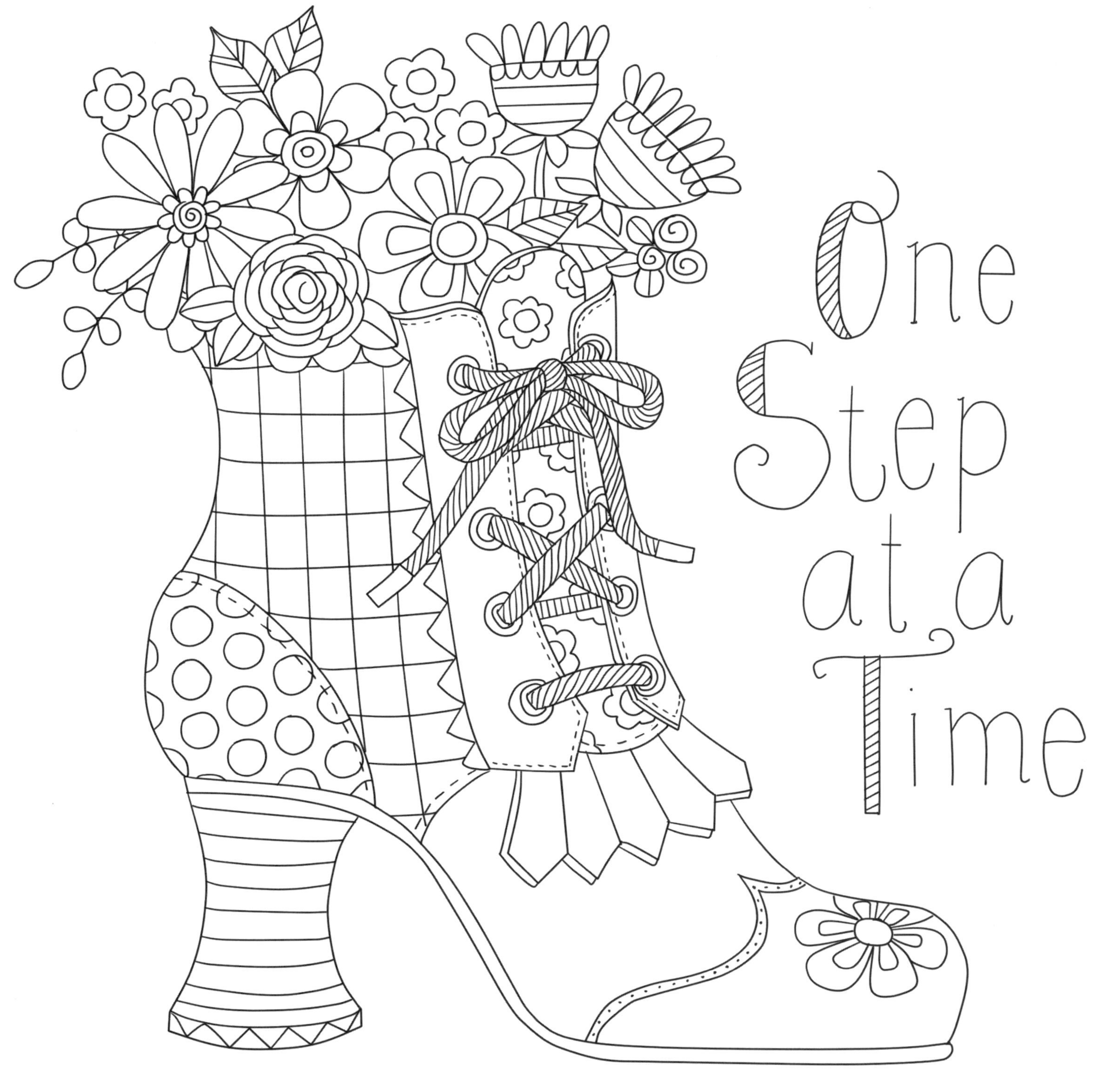
One
Step
at a
Time

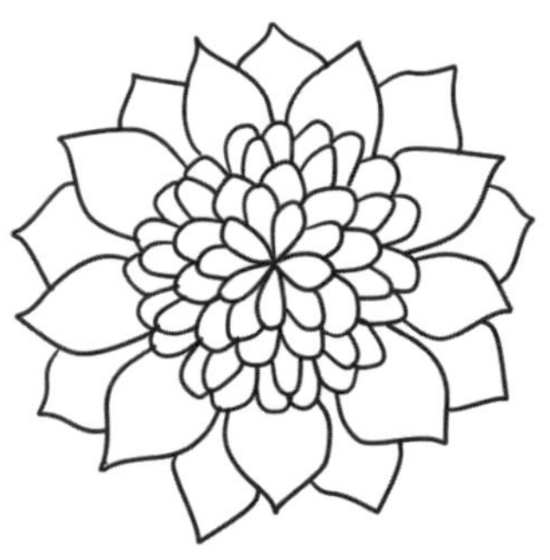

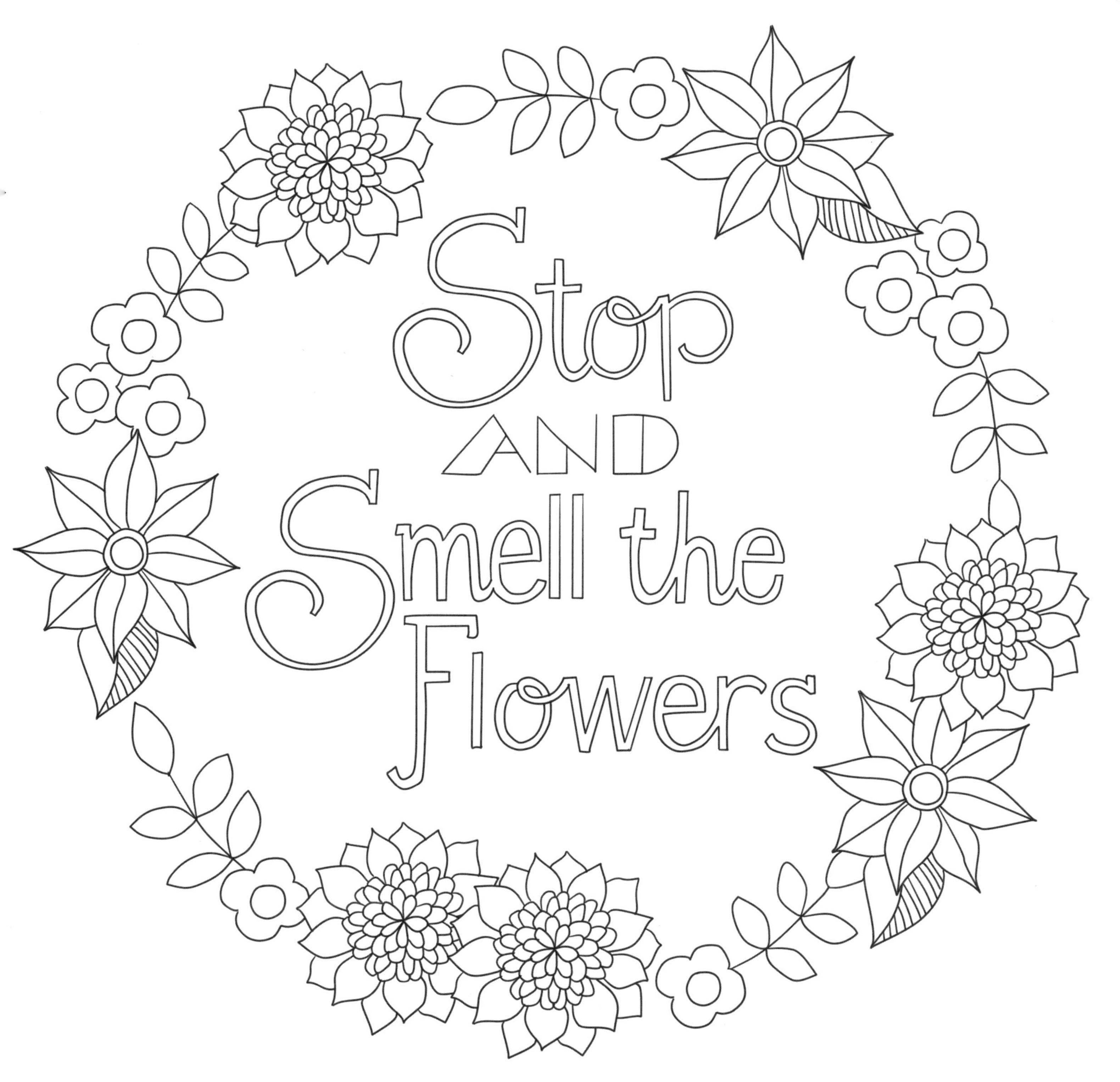
Stop
AND
Smell the
Flowers

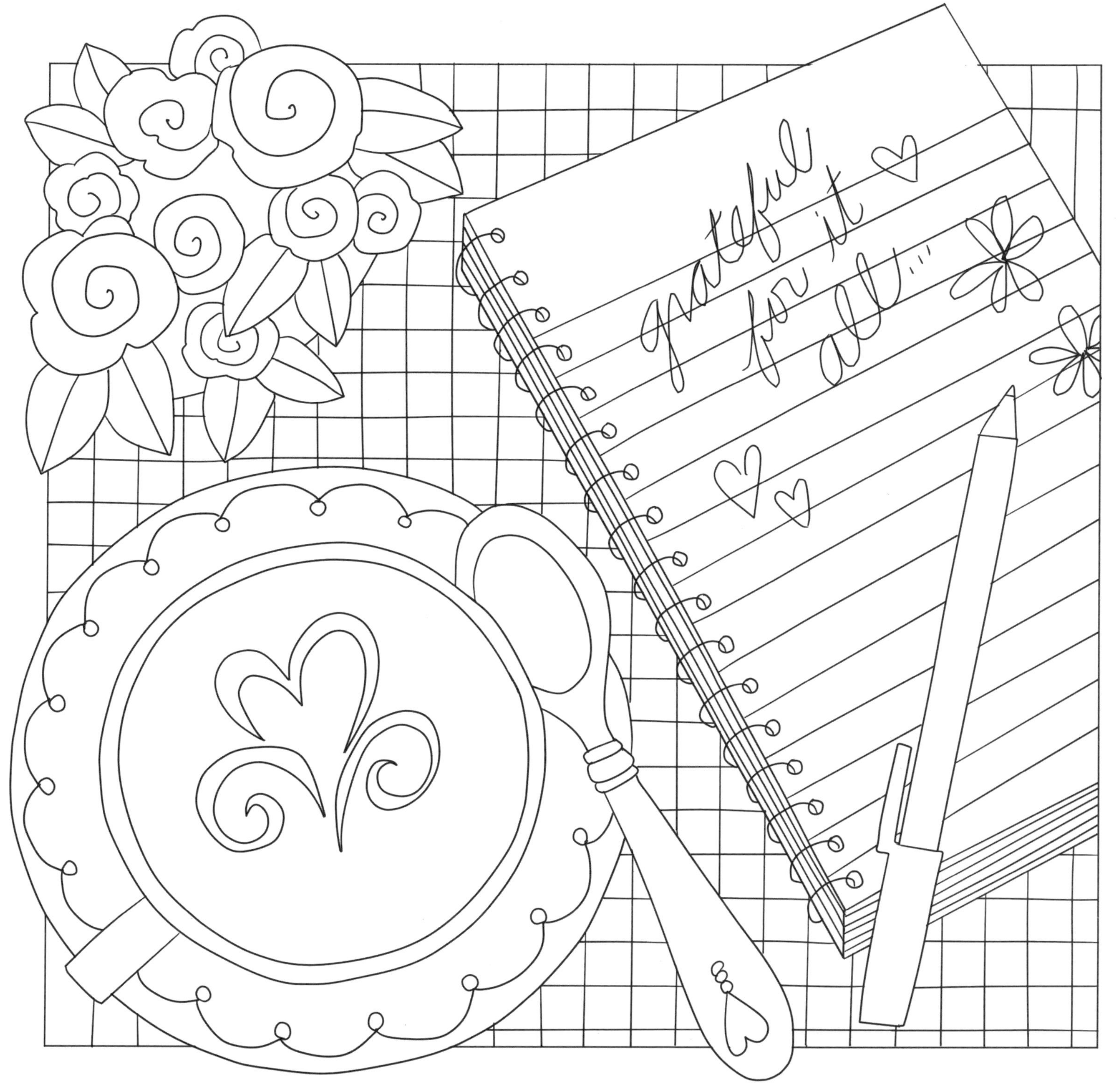
grateful for it all...

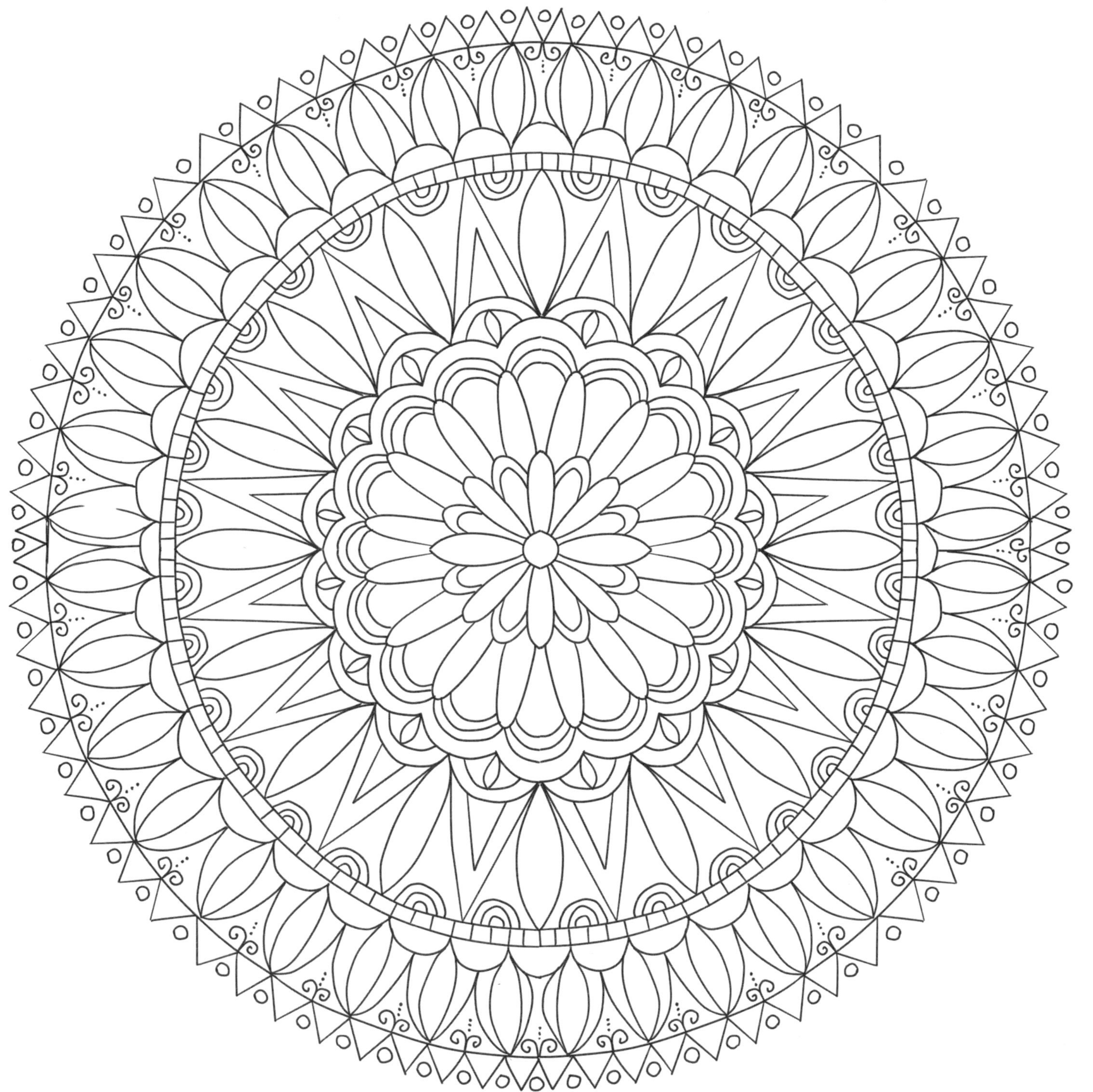

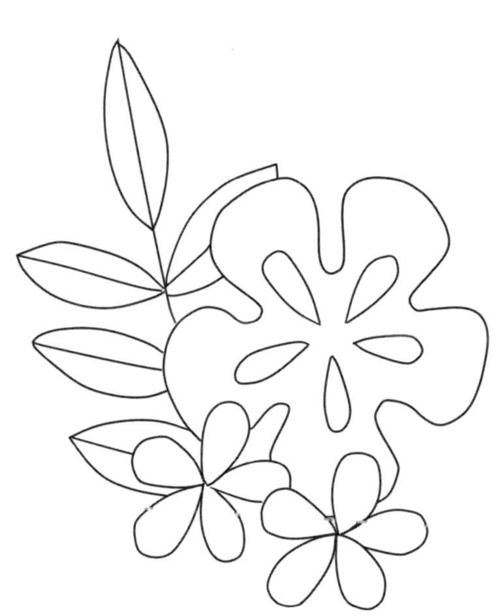

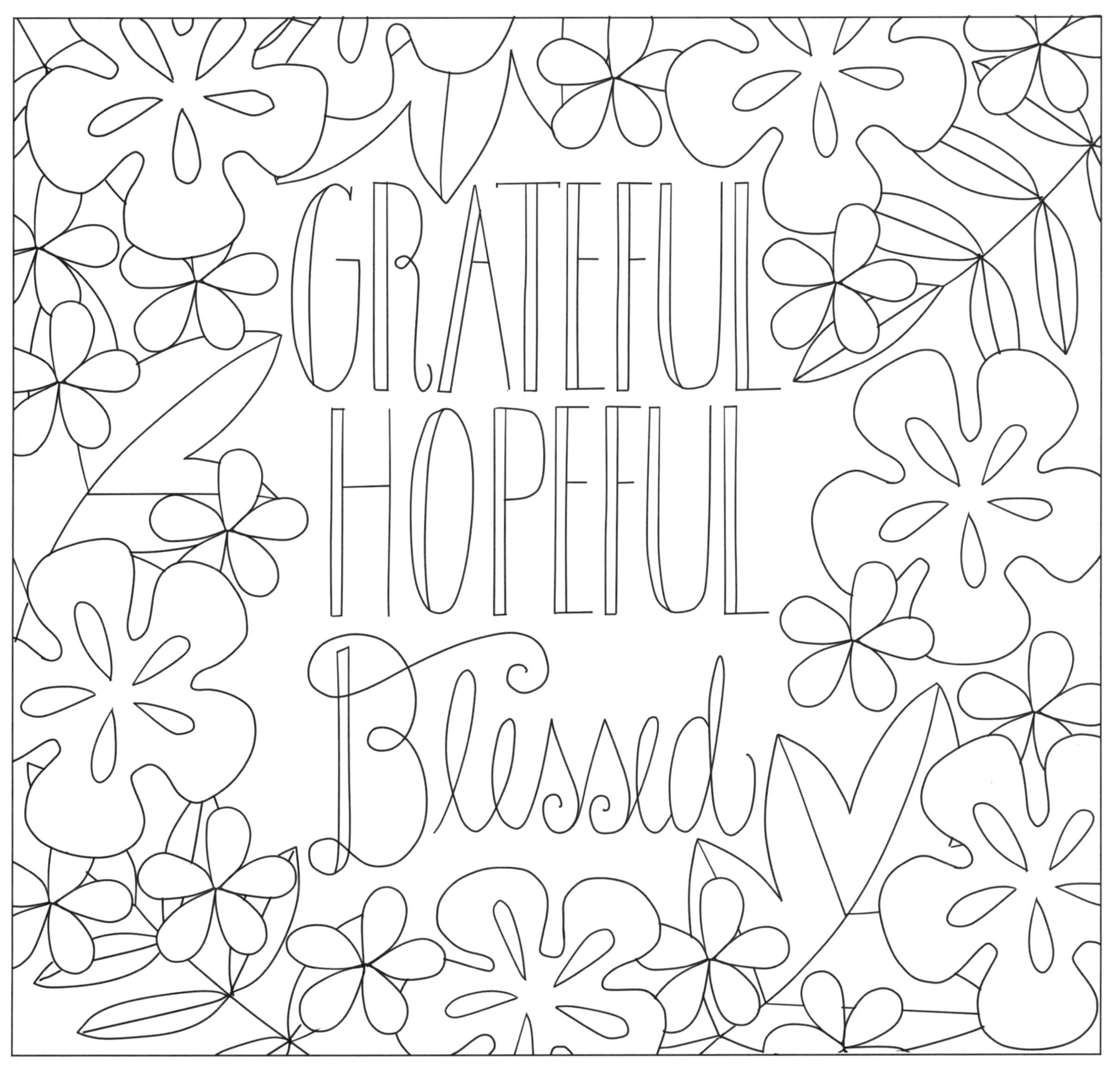
GRATEFUL
HOPEFUL
Blessed

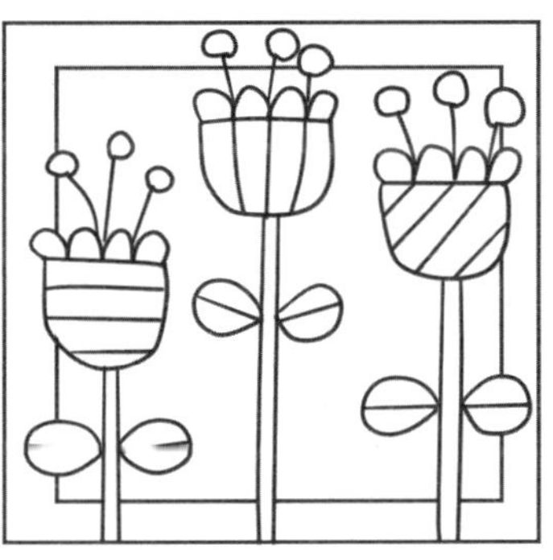

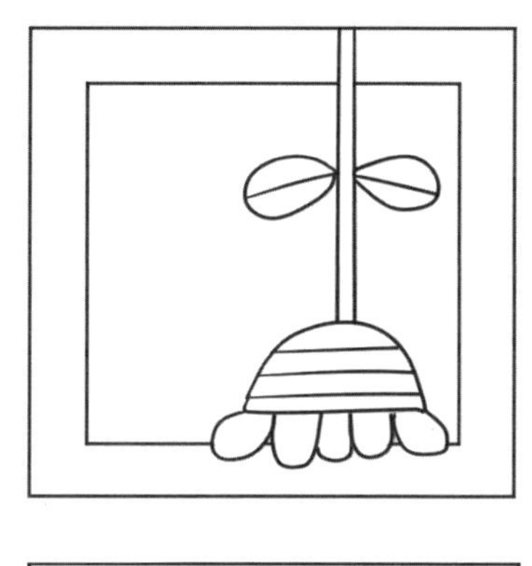
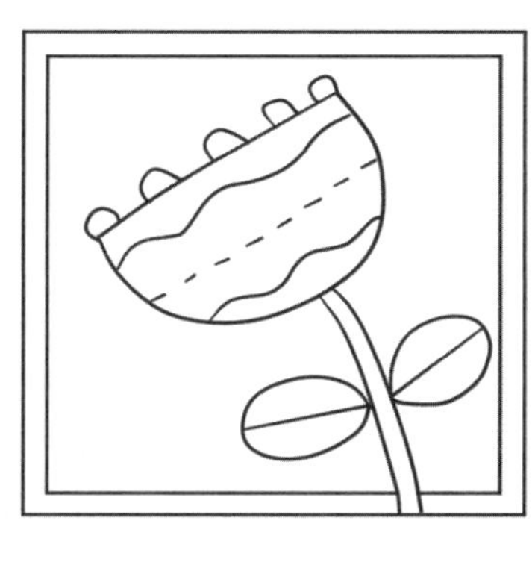
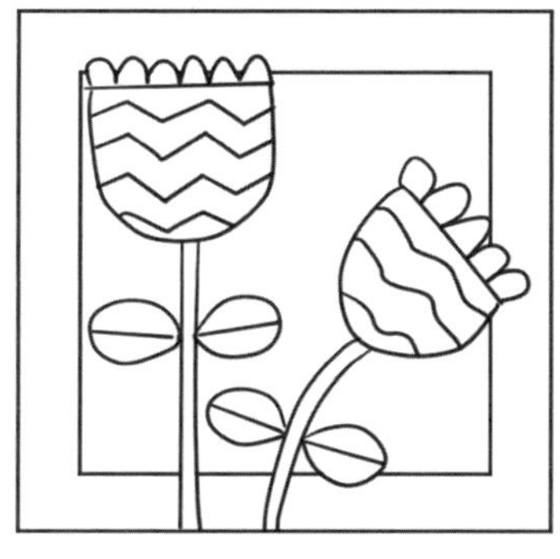
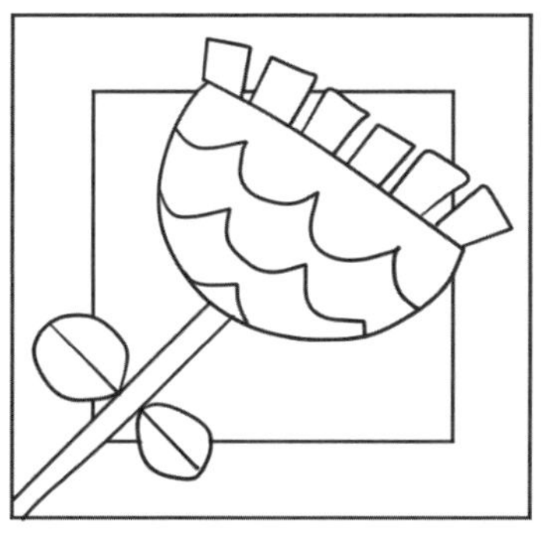
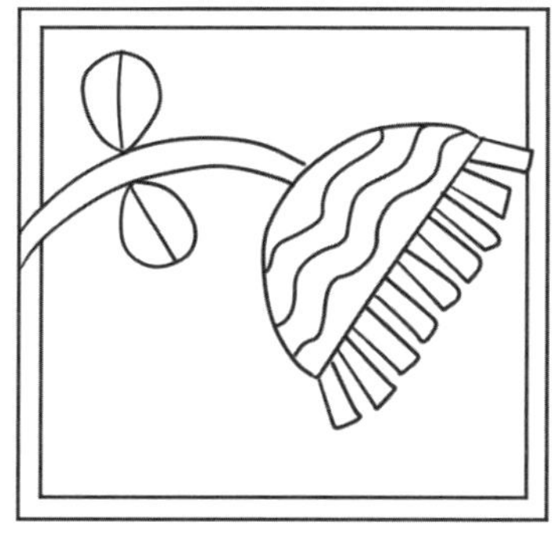
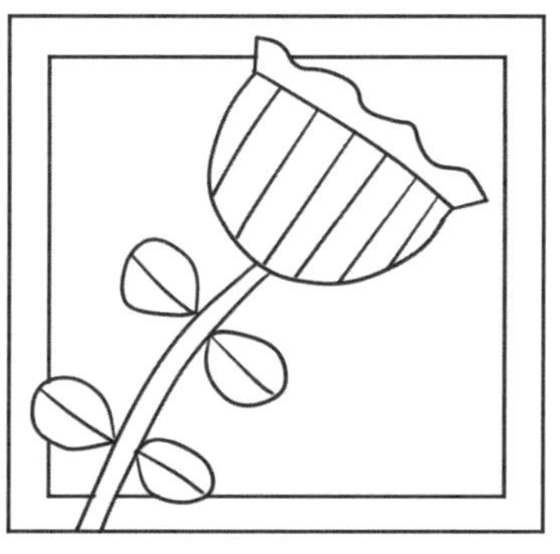
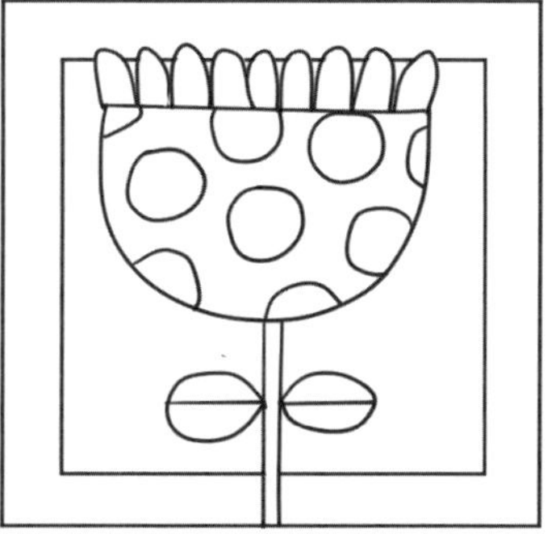
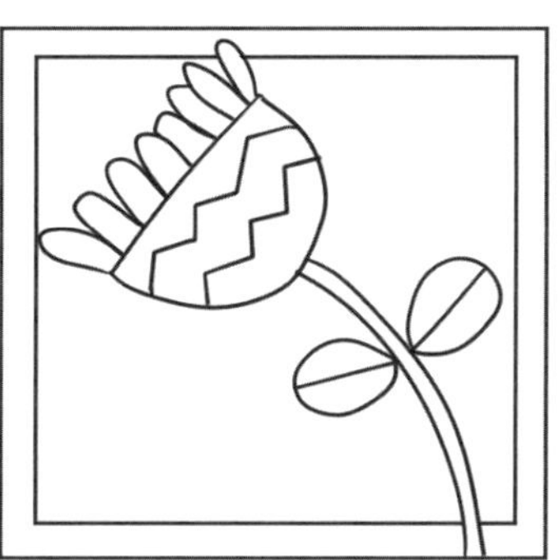
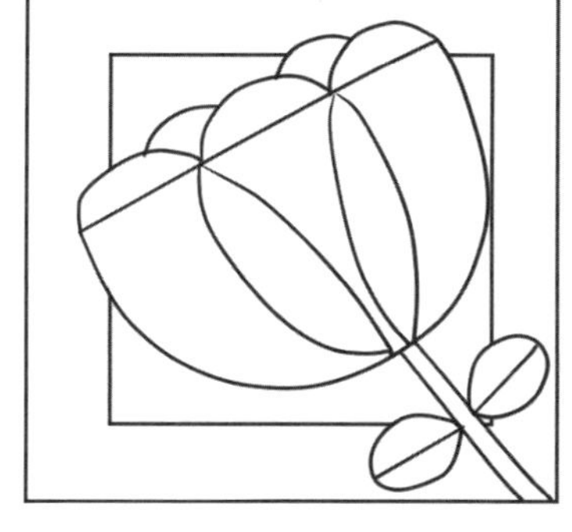
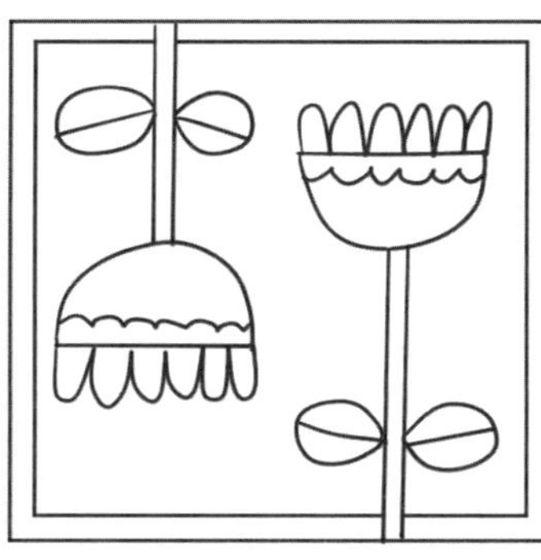
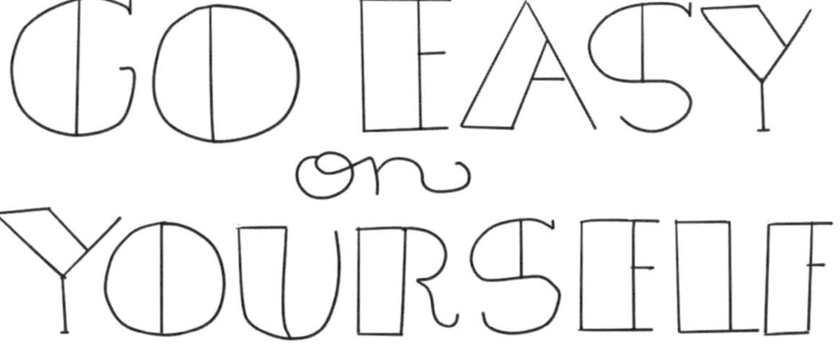
GO EASY on YOURSELF
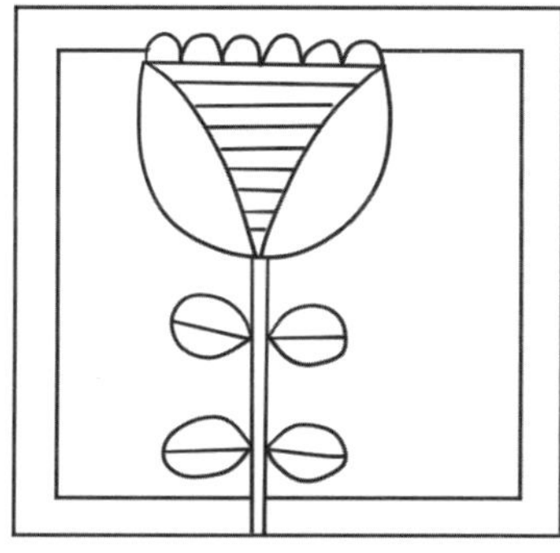
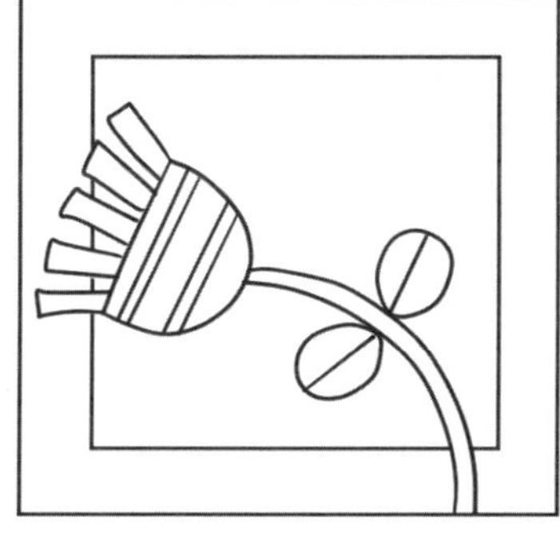
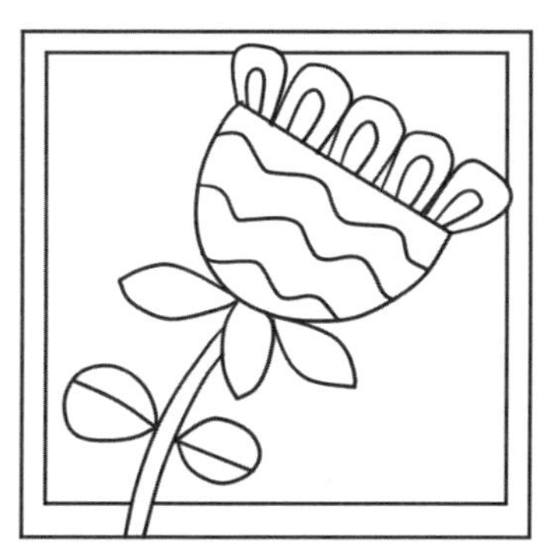
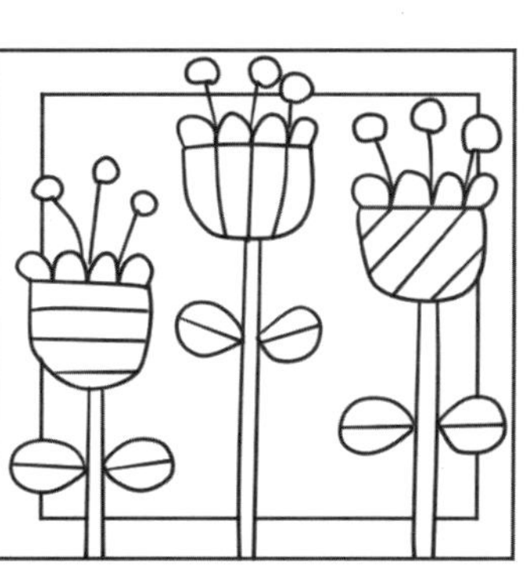

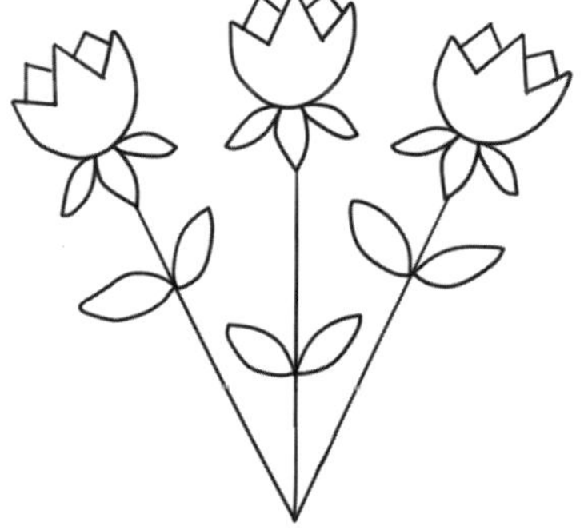

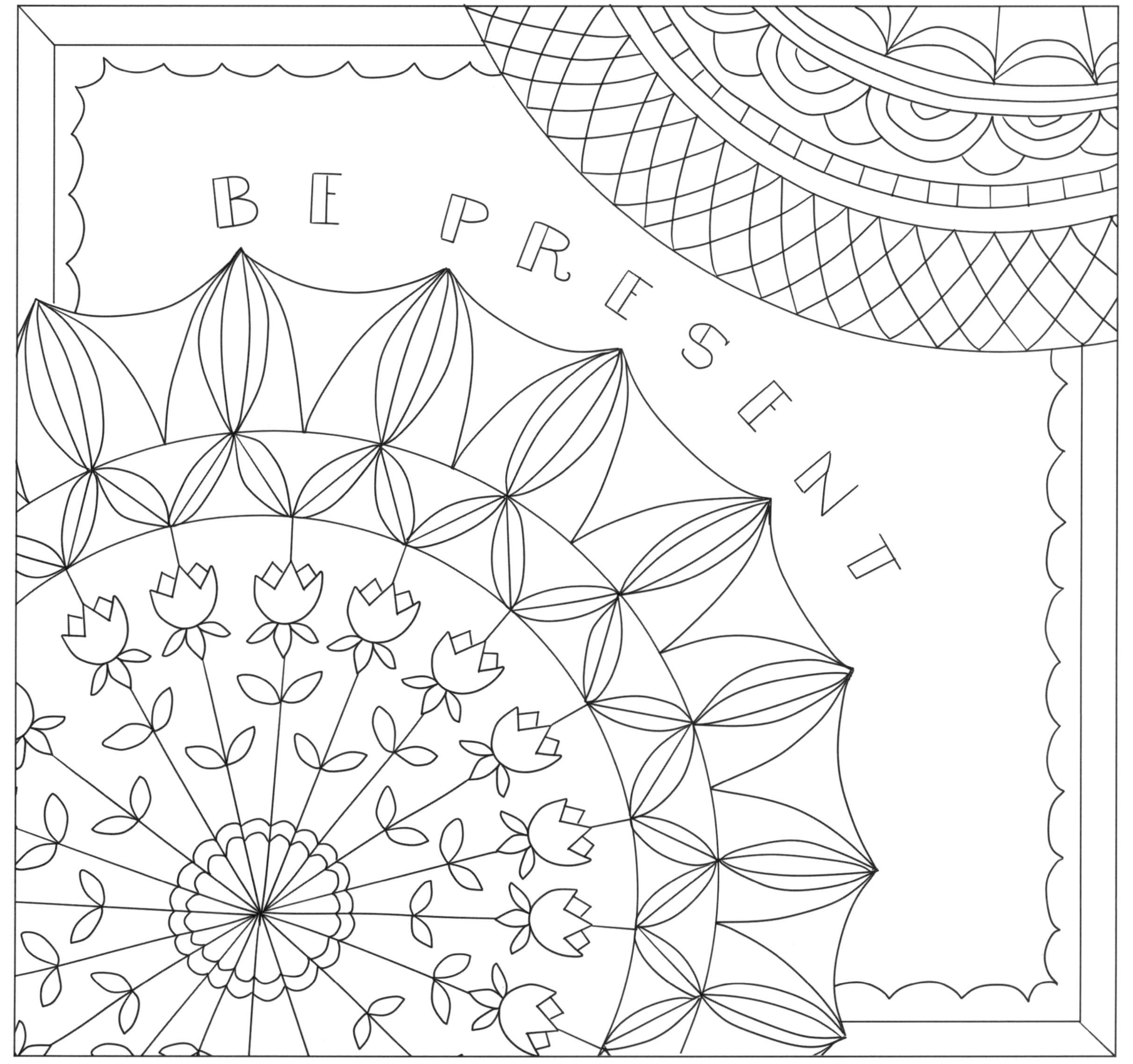
BE PRESENT

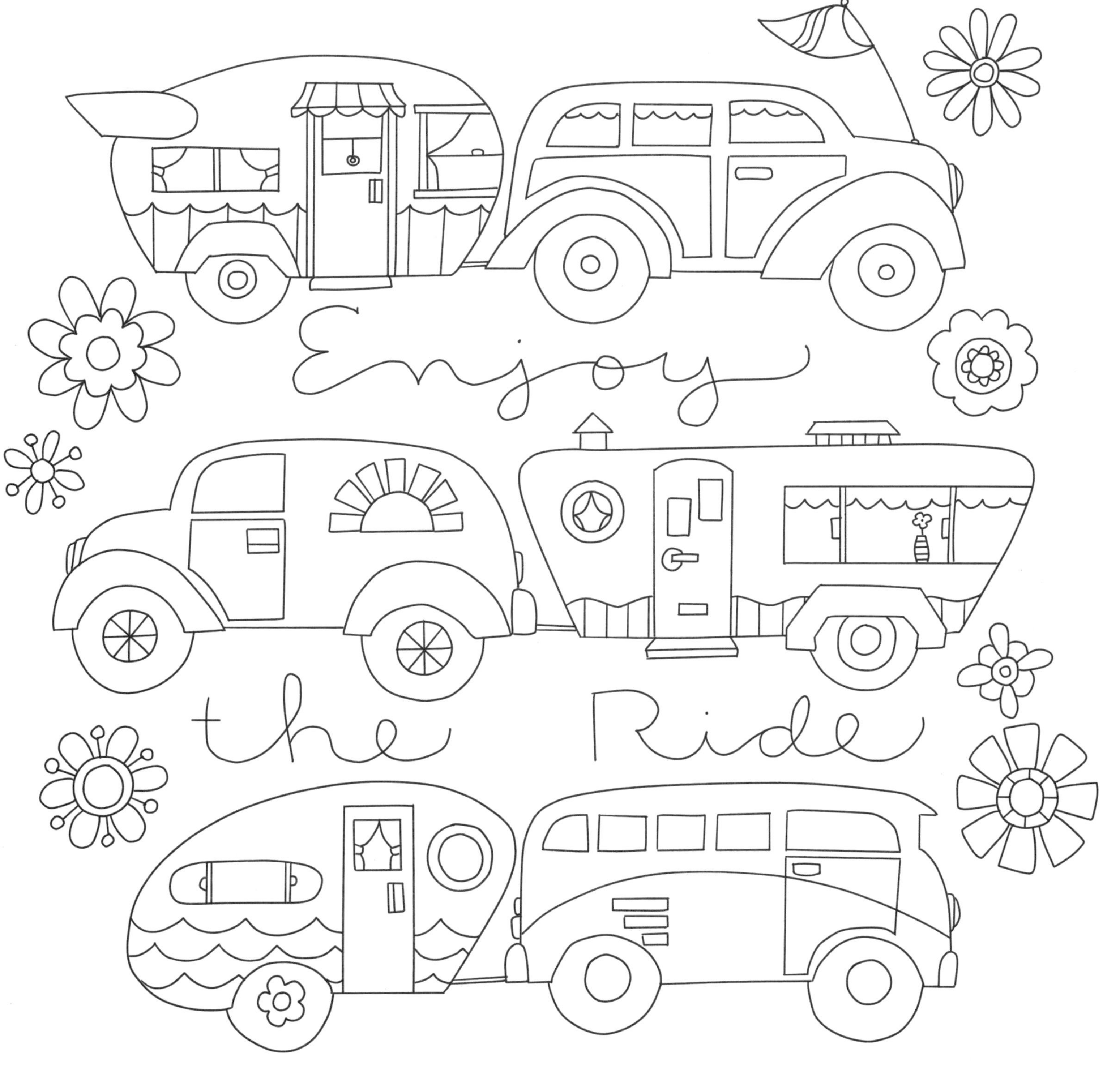
Enjoy
the Ride

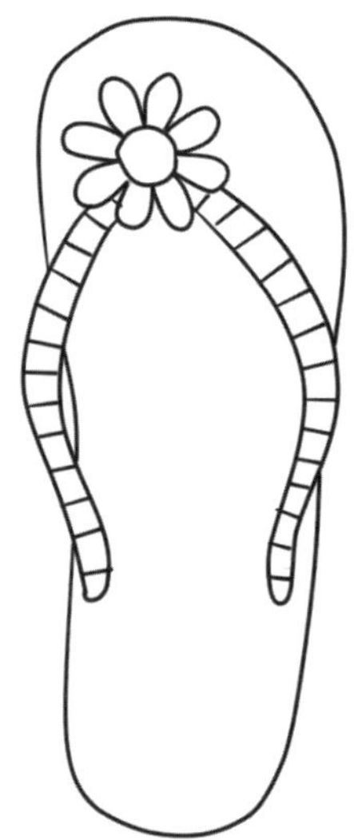

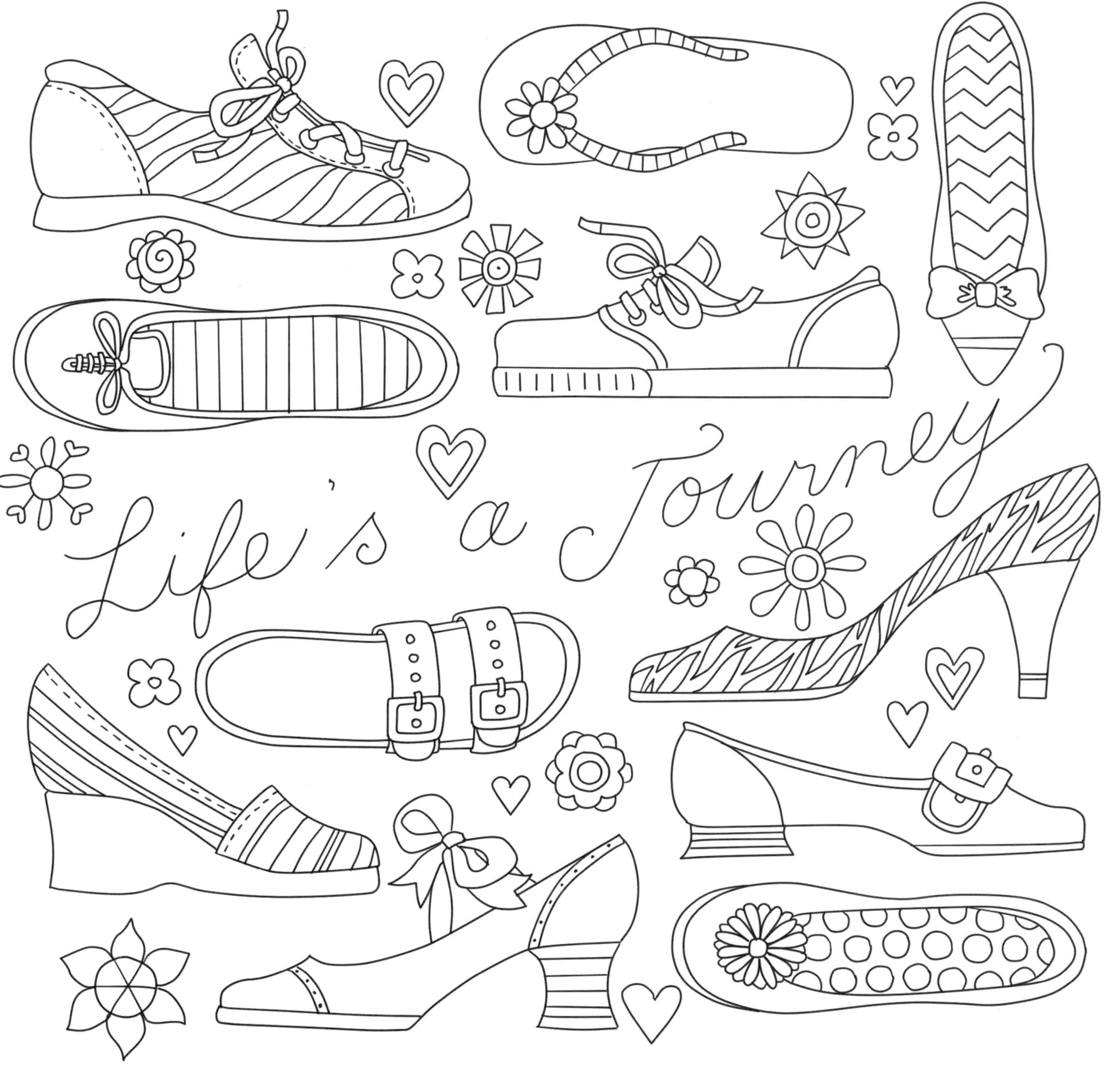
Life's a Journey

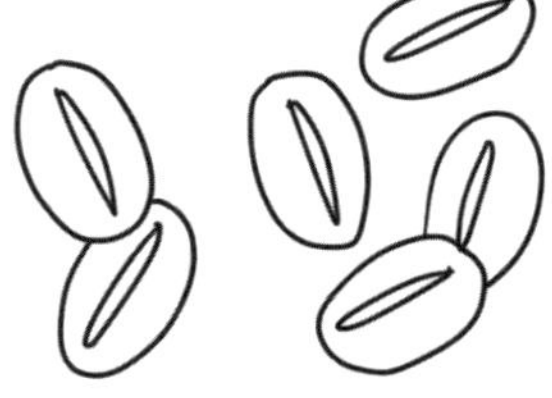

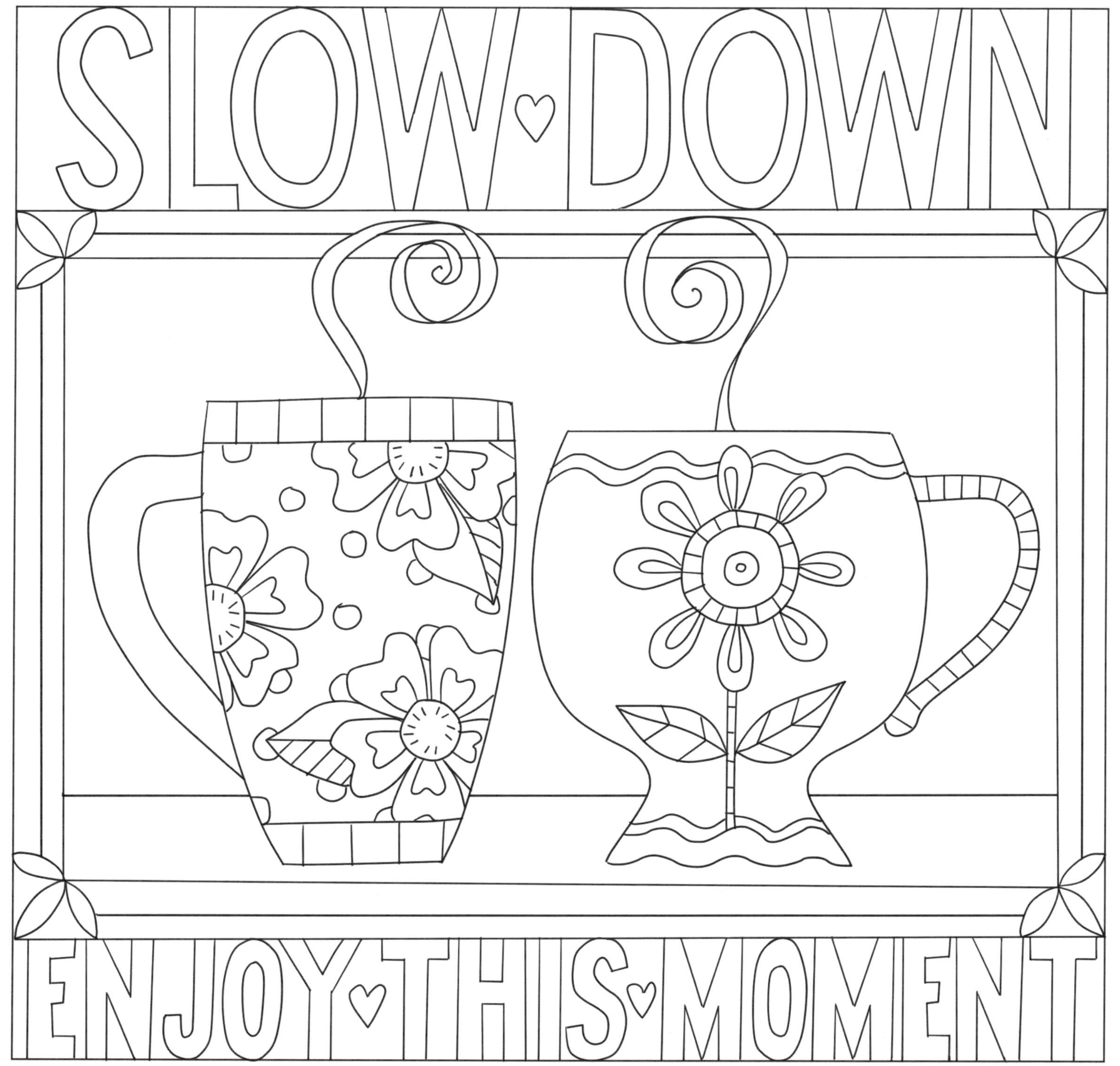
SLOW DOWN
ENJOY THIS MOMENT

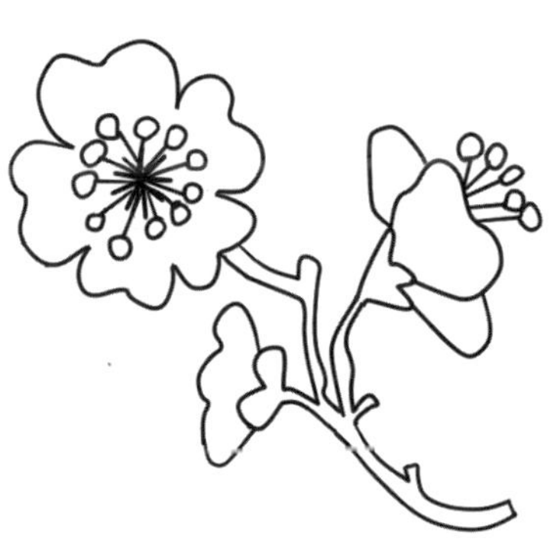

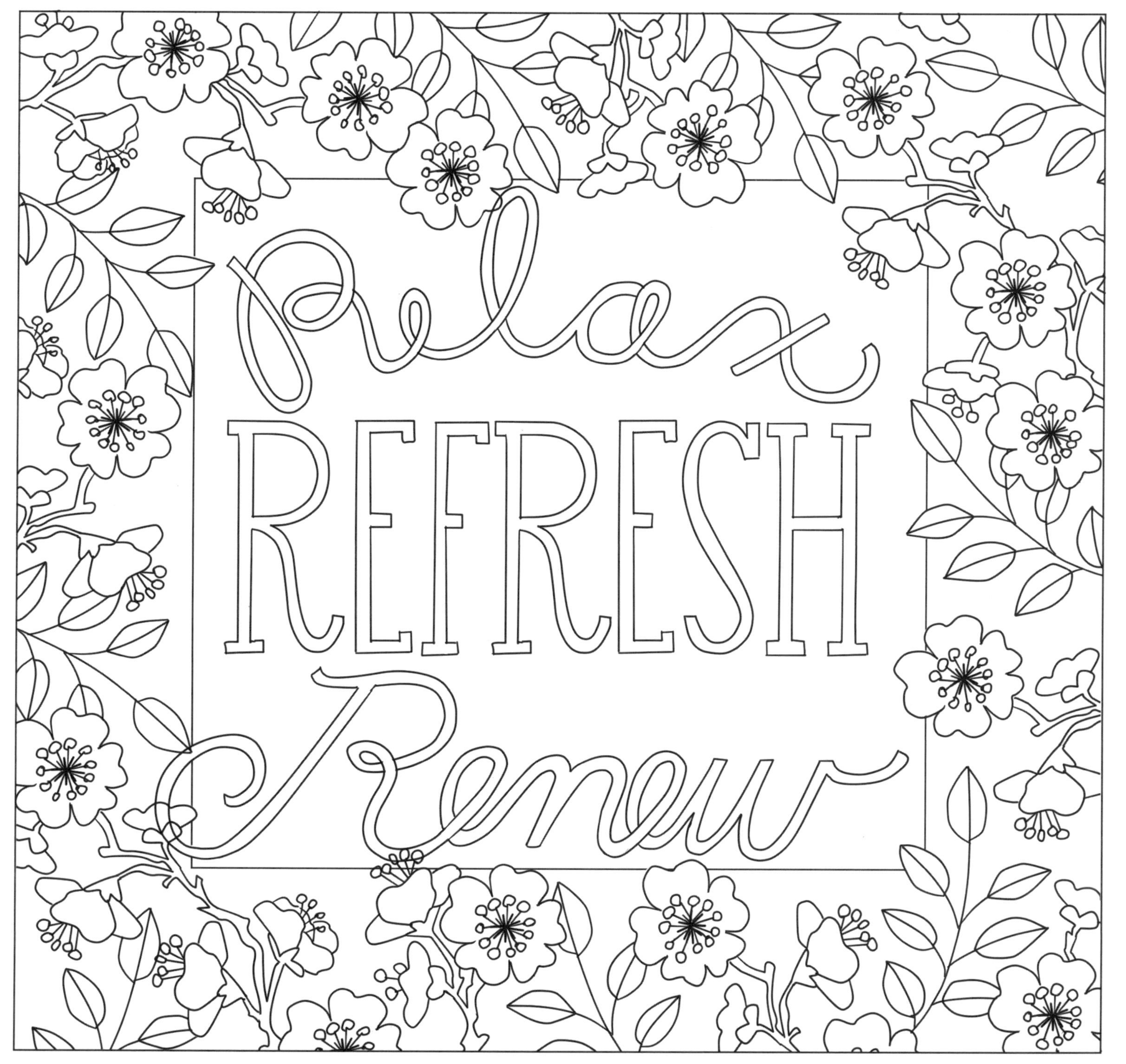
Relax
REFRESH
Renew

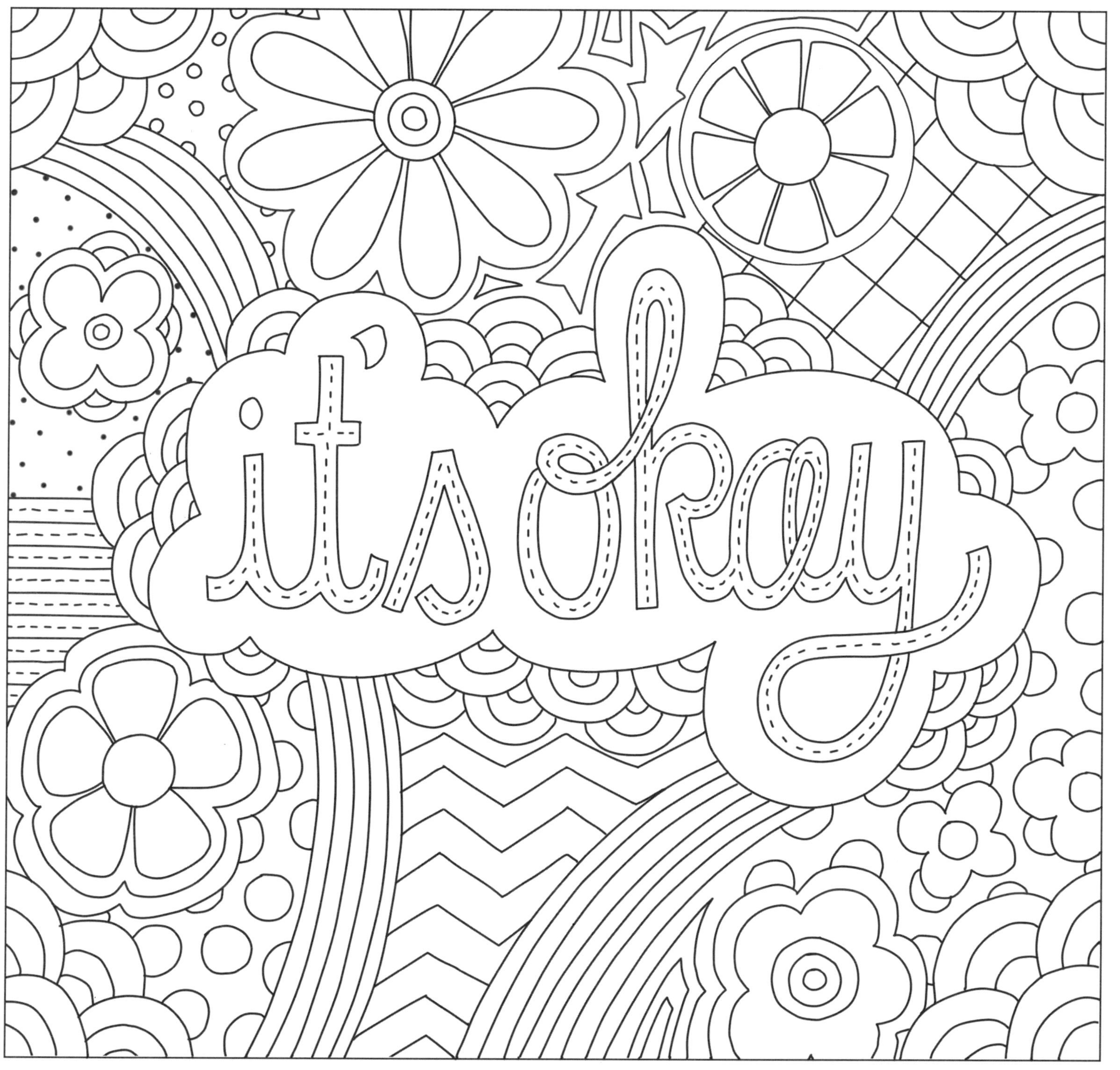
it's okay

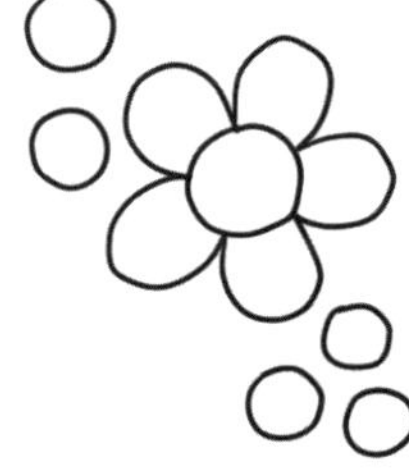

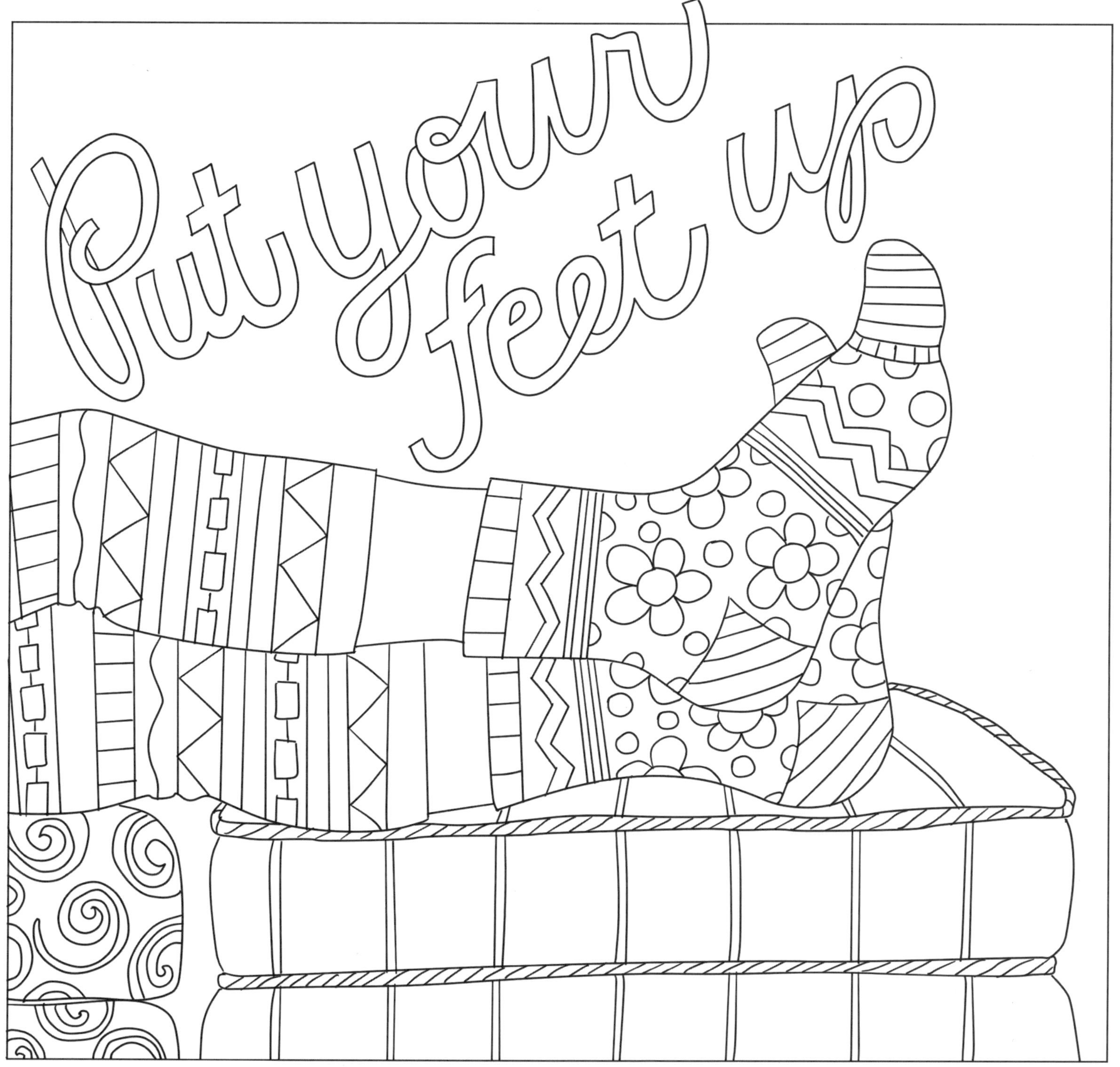
Put your feet up

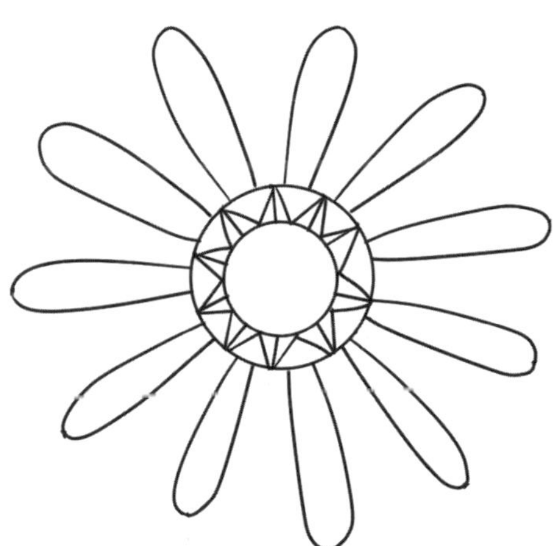

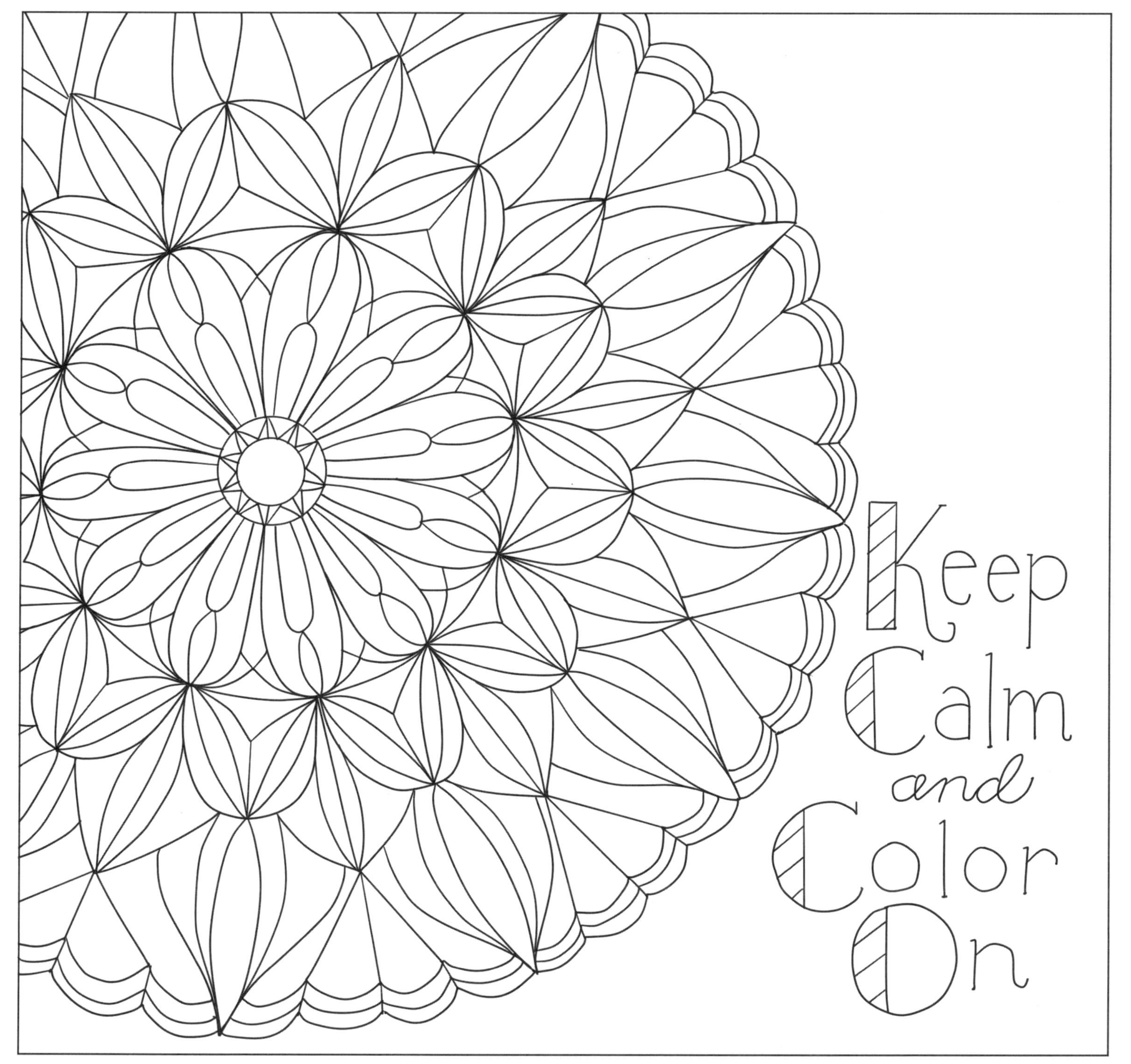
Keep
Calm
and
Color
On

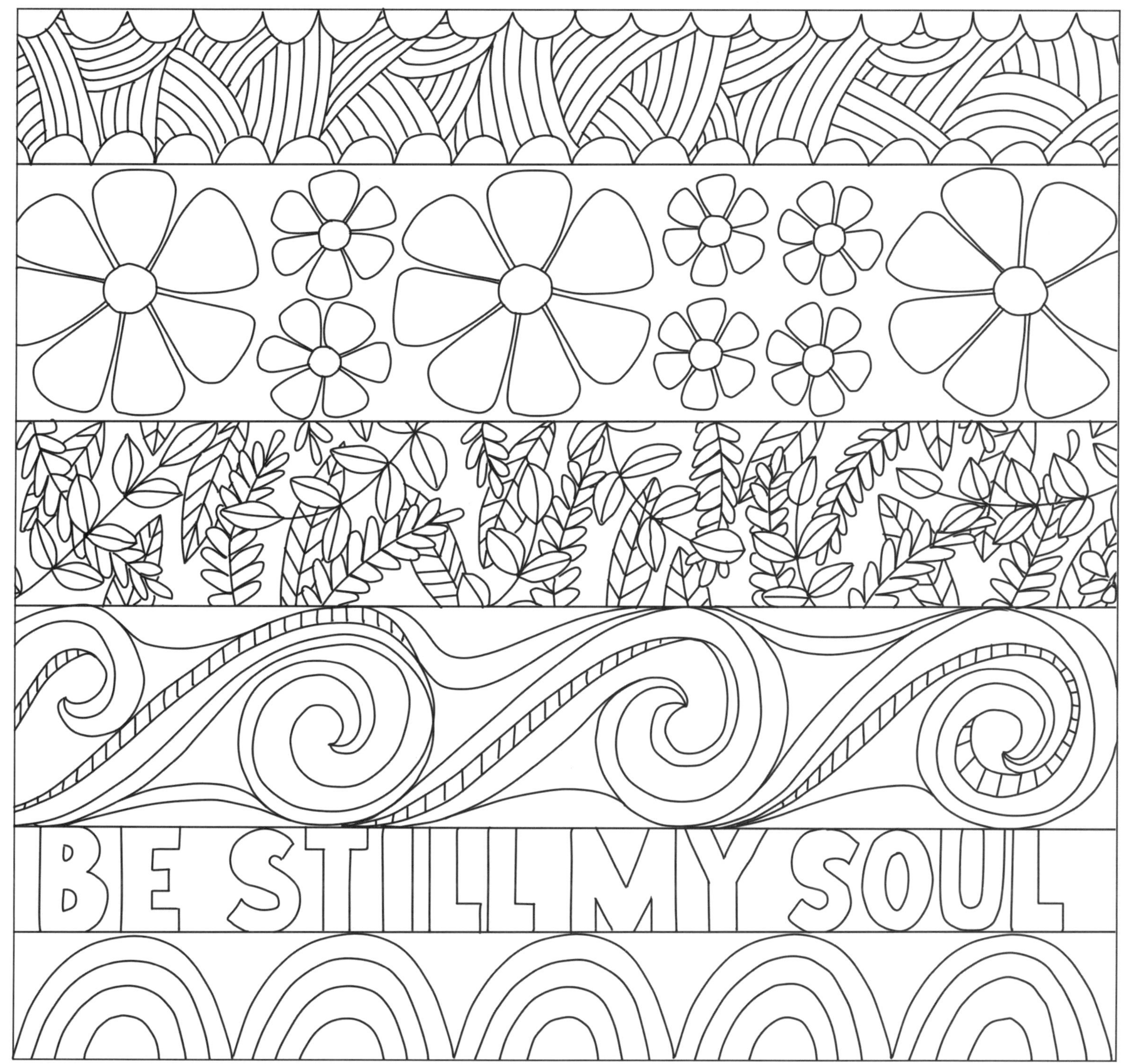
BE STILL MY SOUL

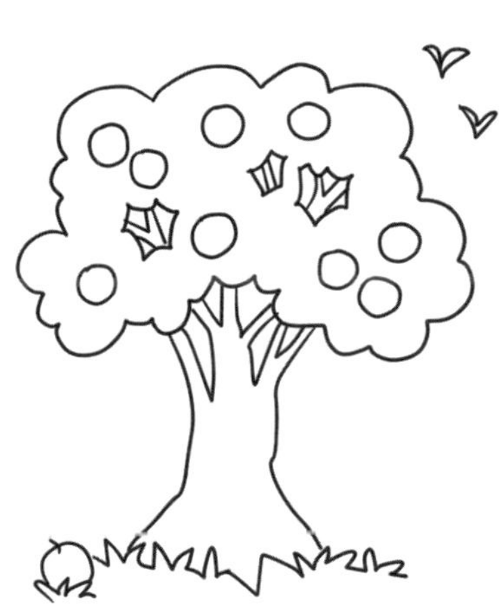

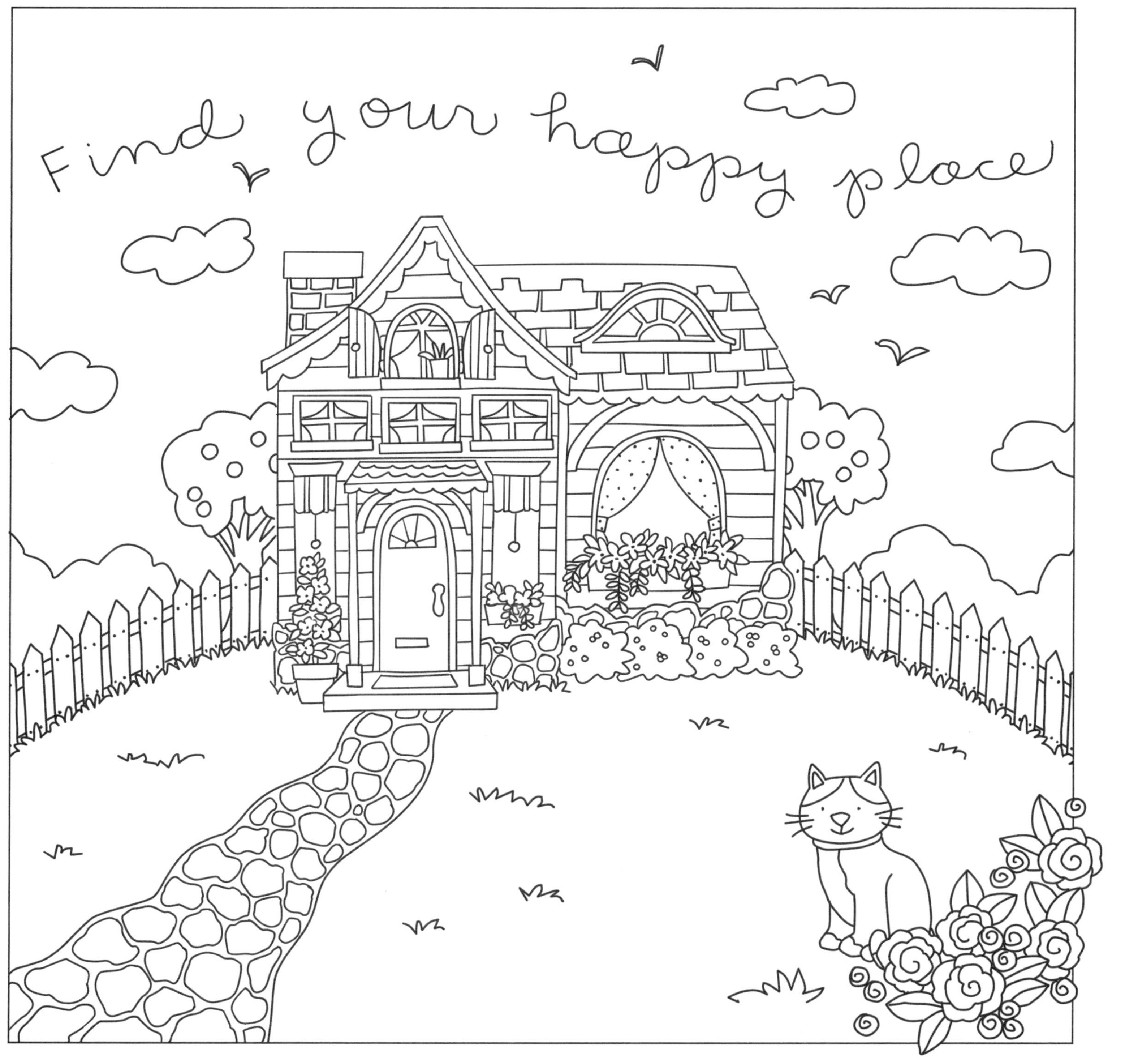
Find your happy place

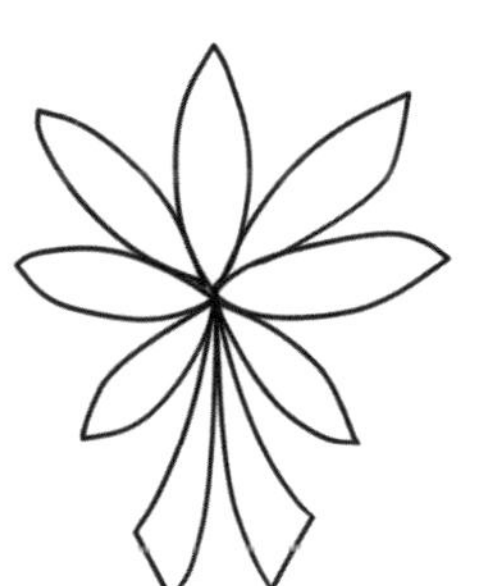

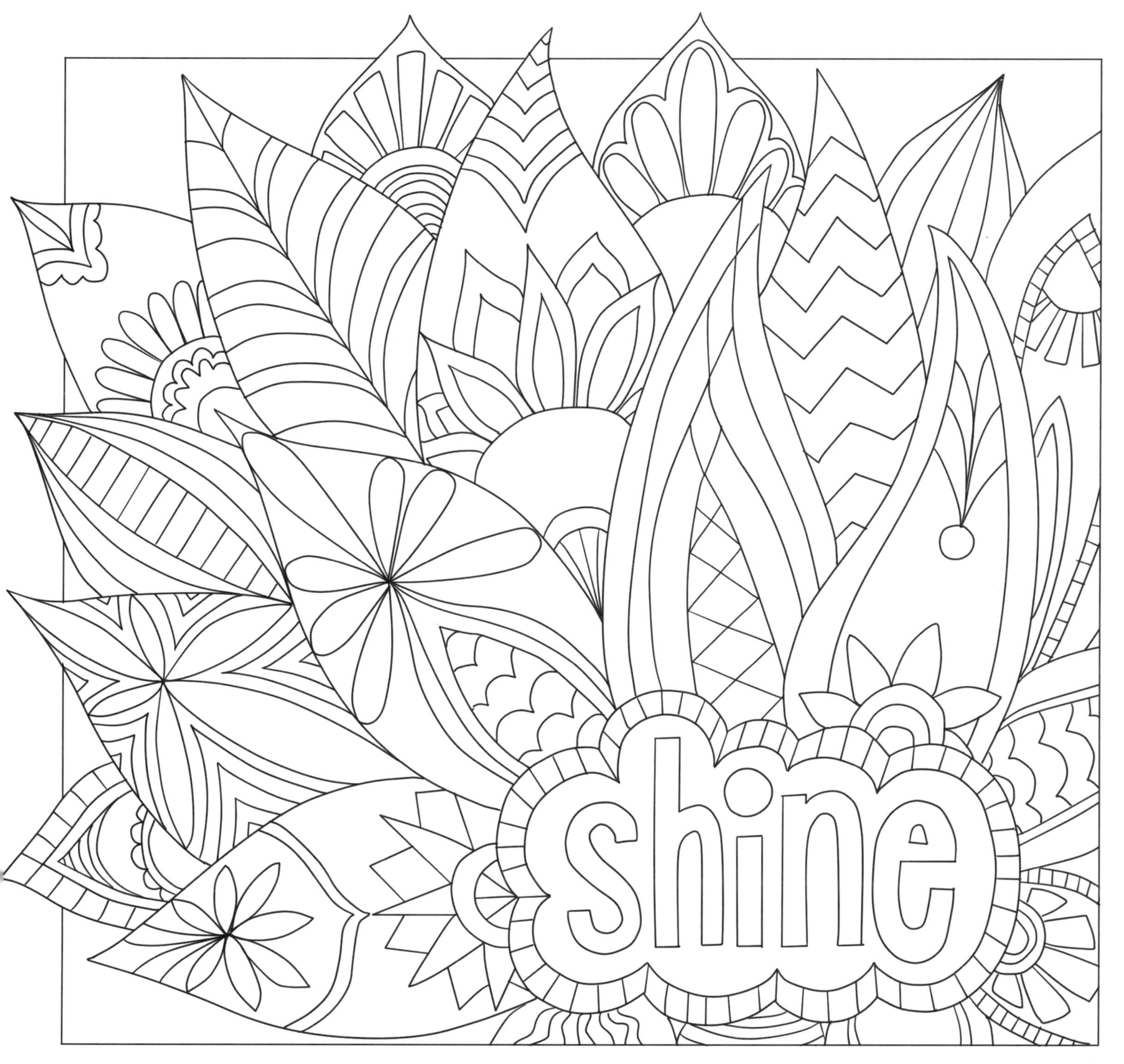
shine

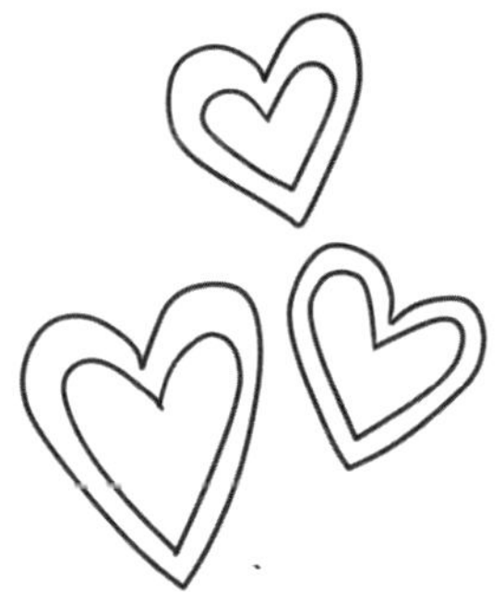

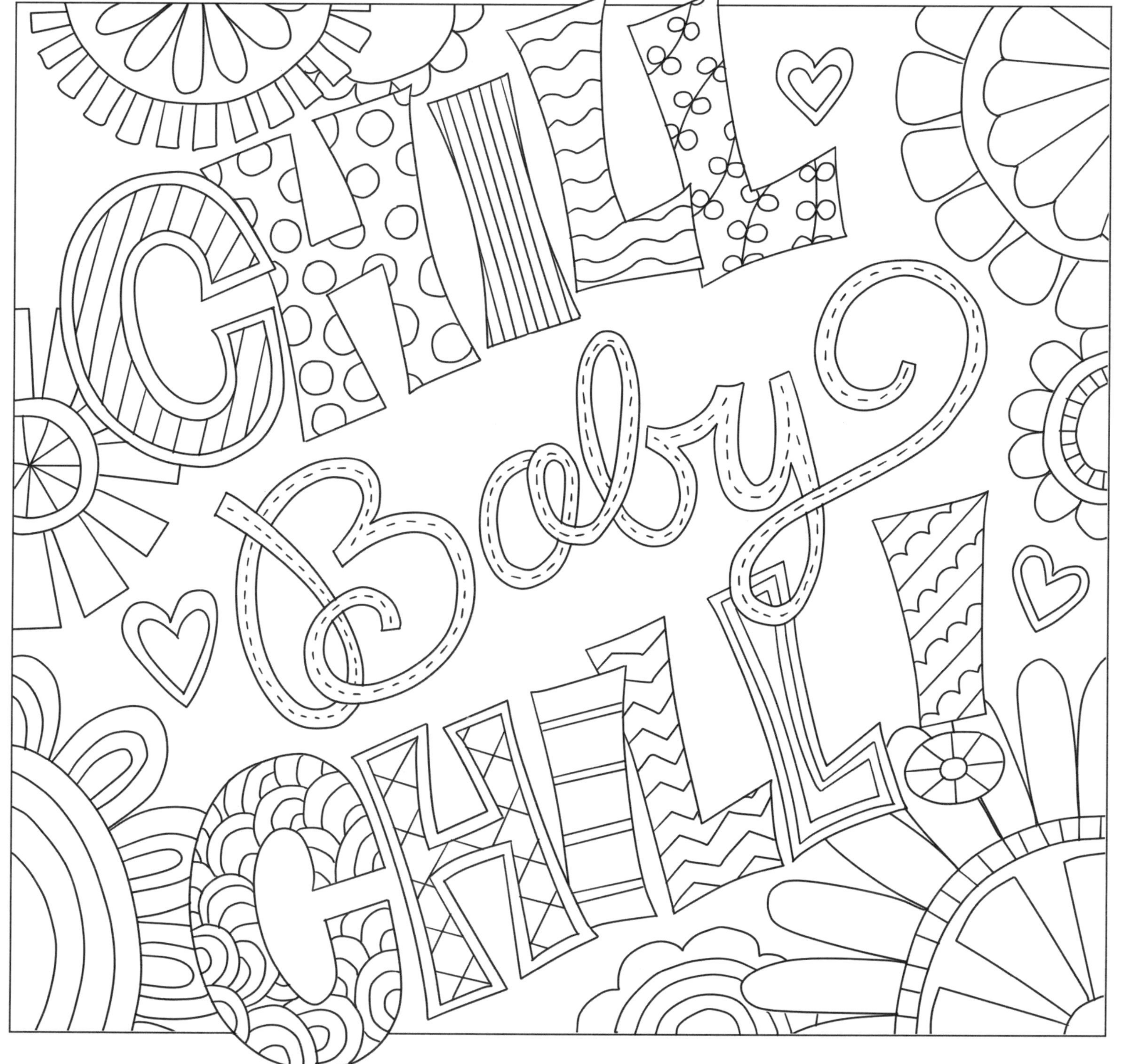
Chill
Baby
Chill

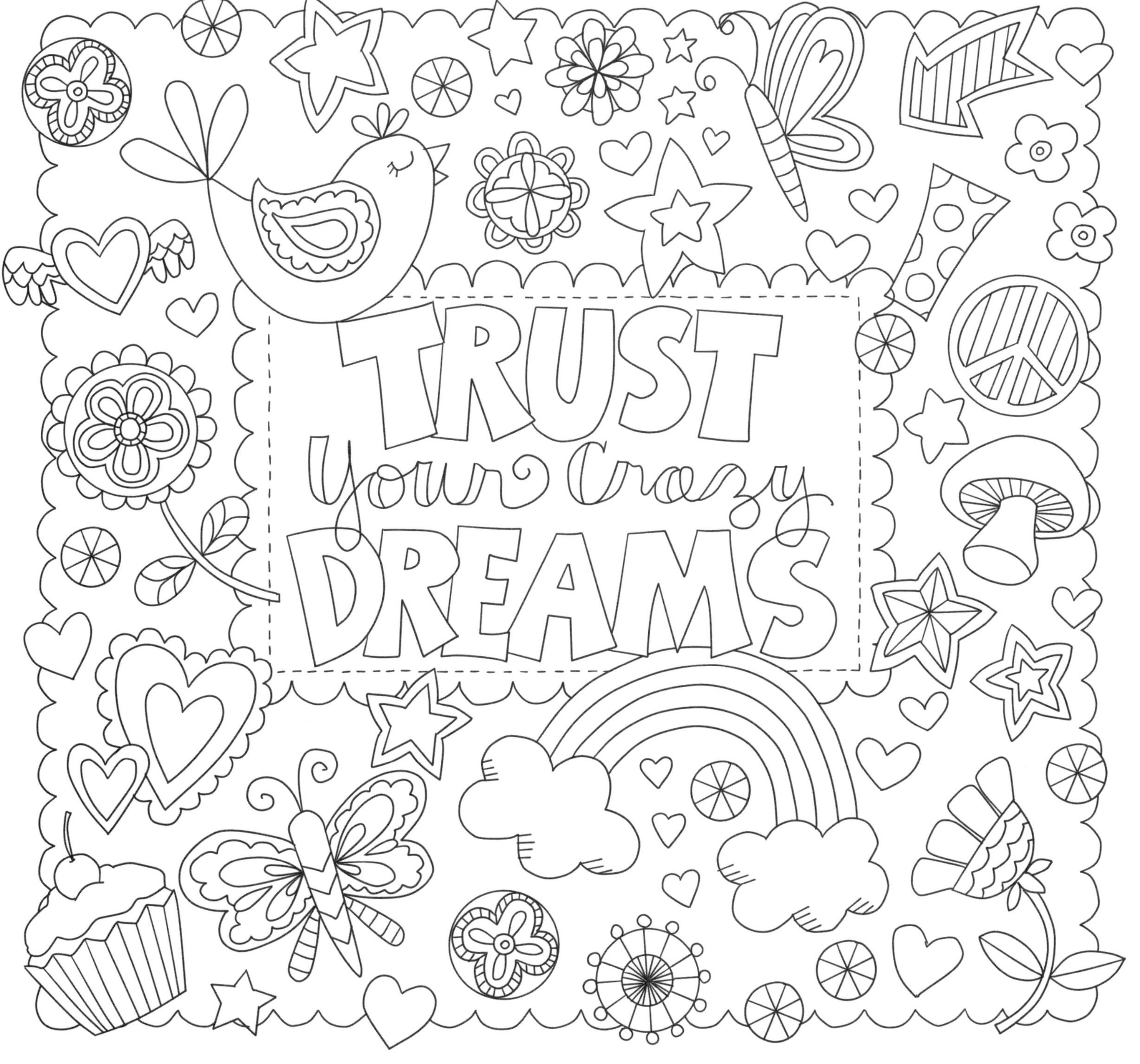
TRUST
Your Crazy
DREAMS

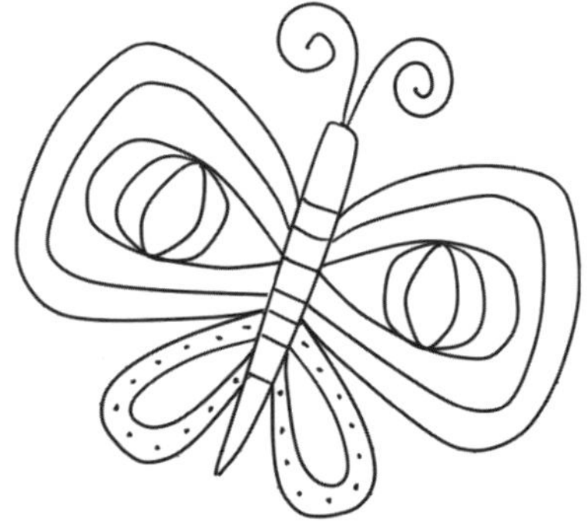

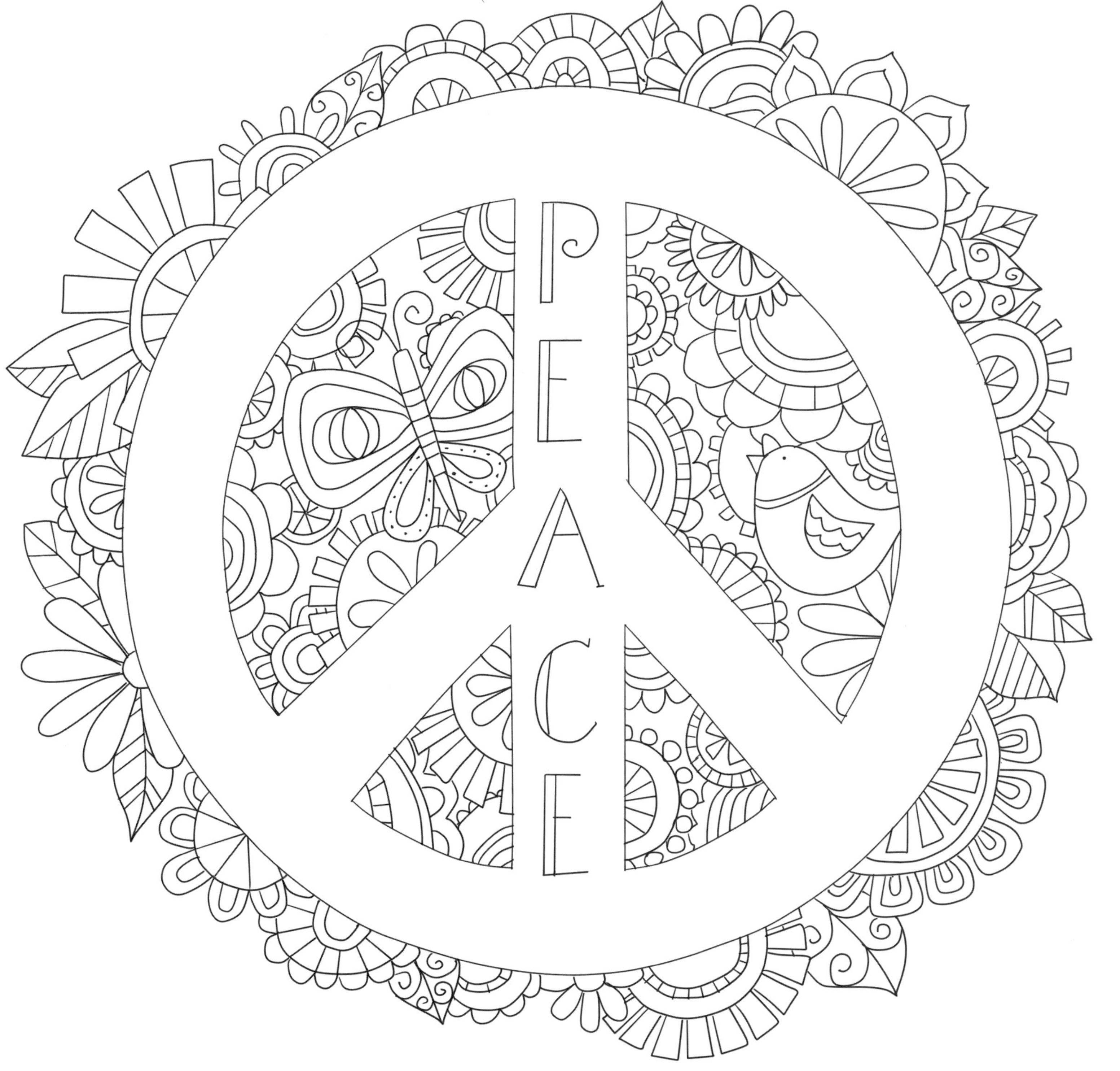
PEACE

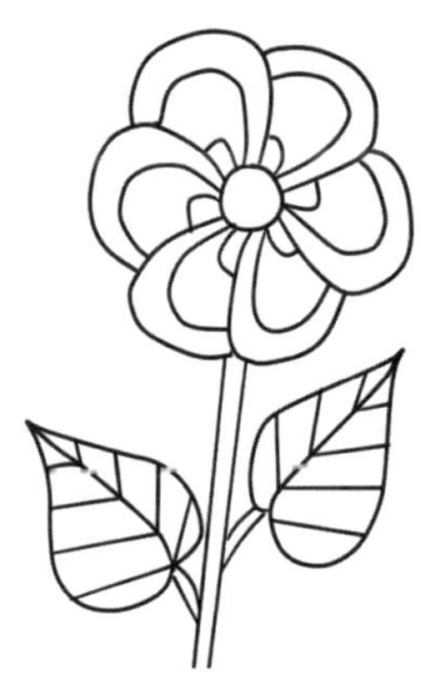

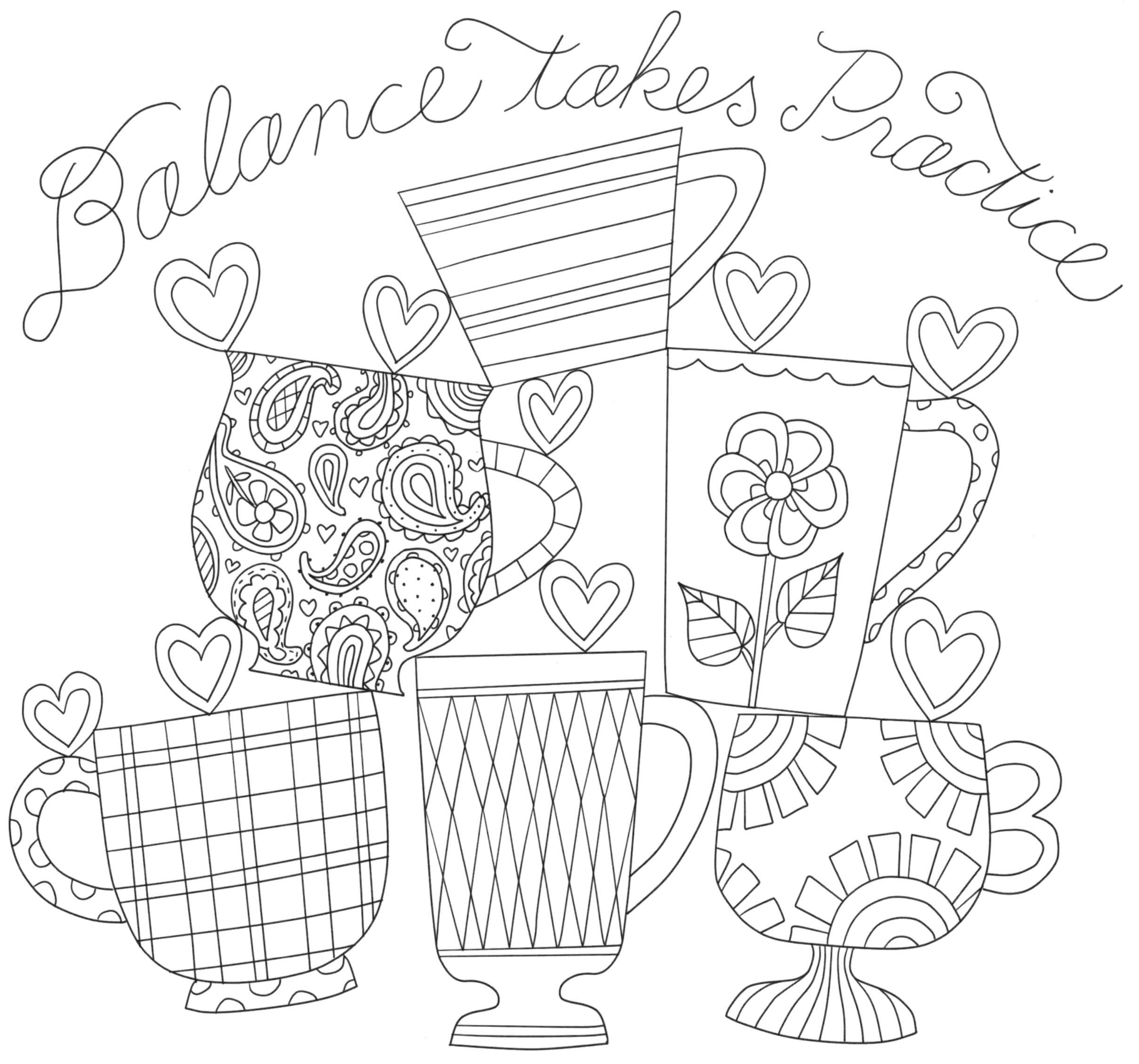
Balance Takes Practice

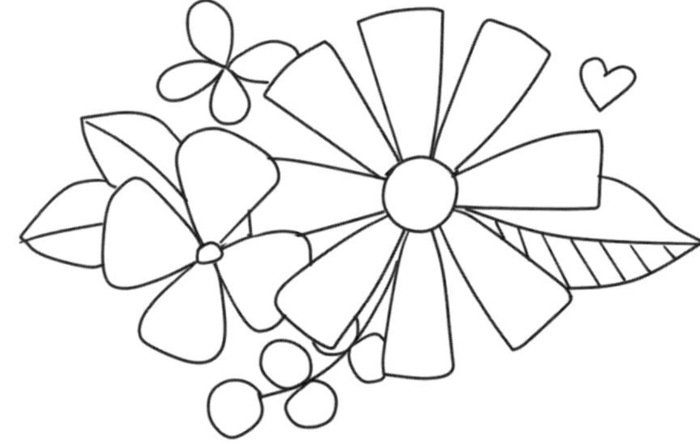

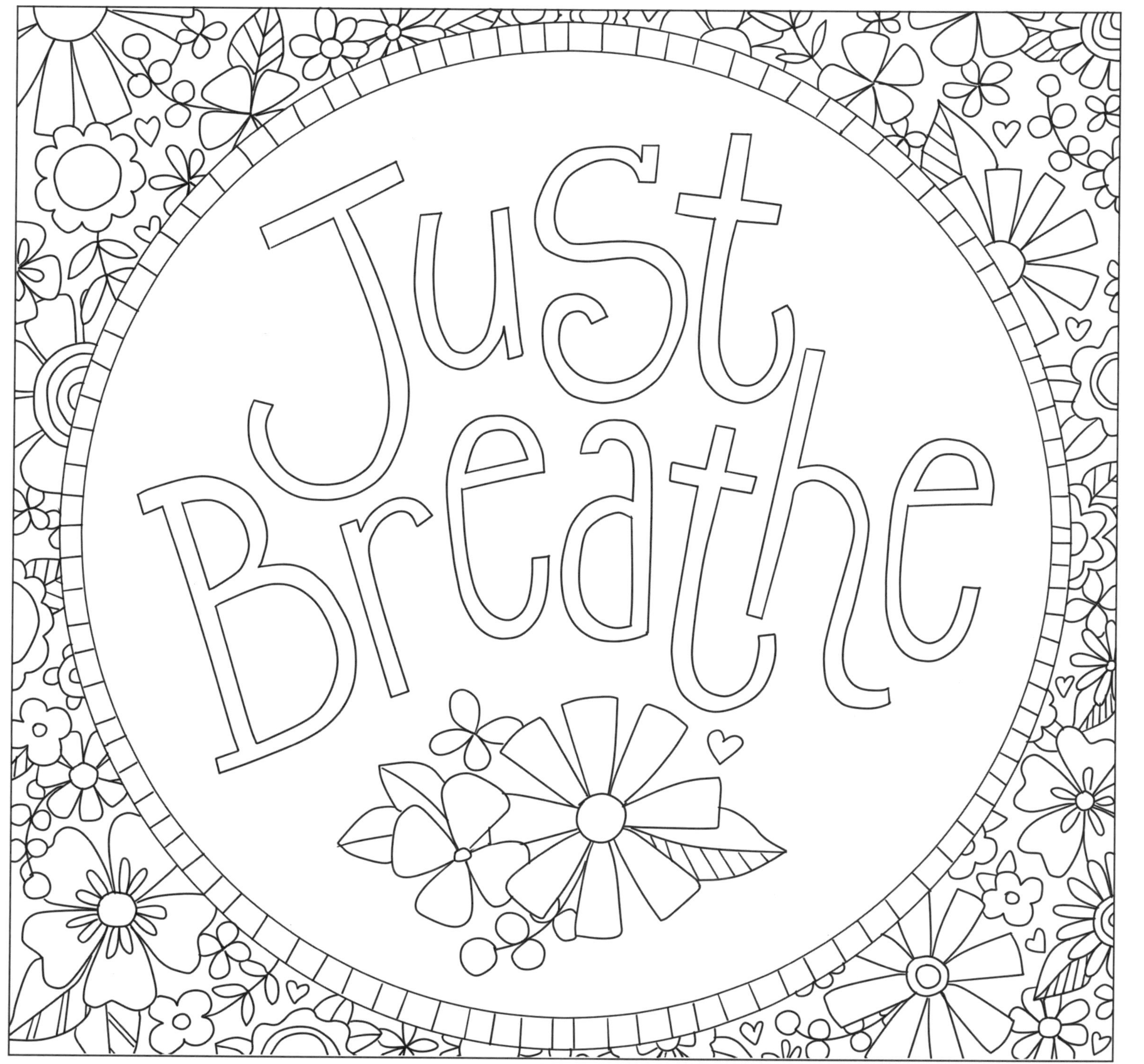
Just
Breathe

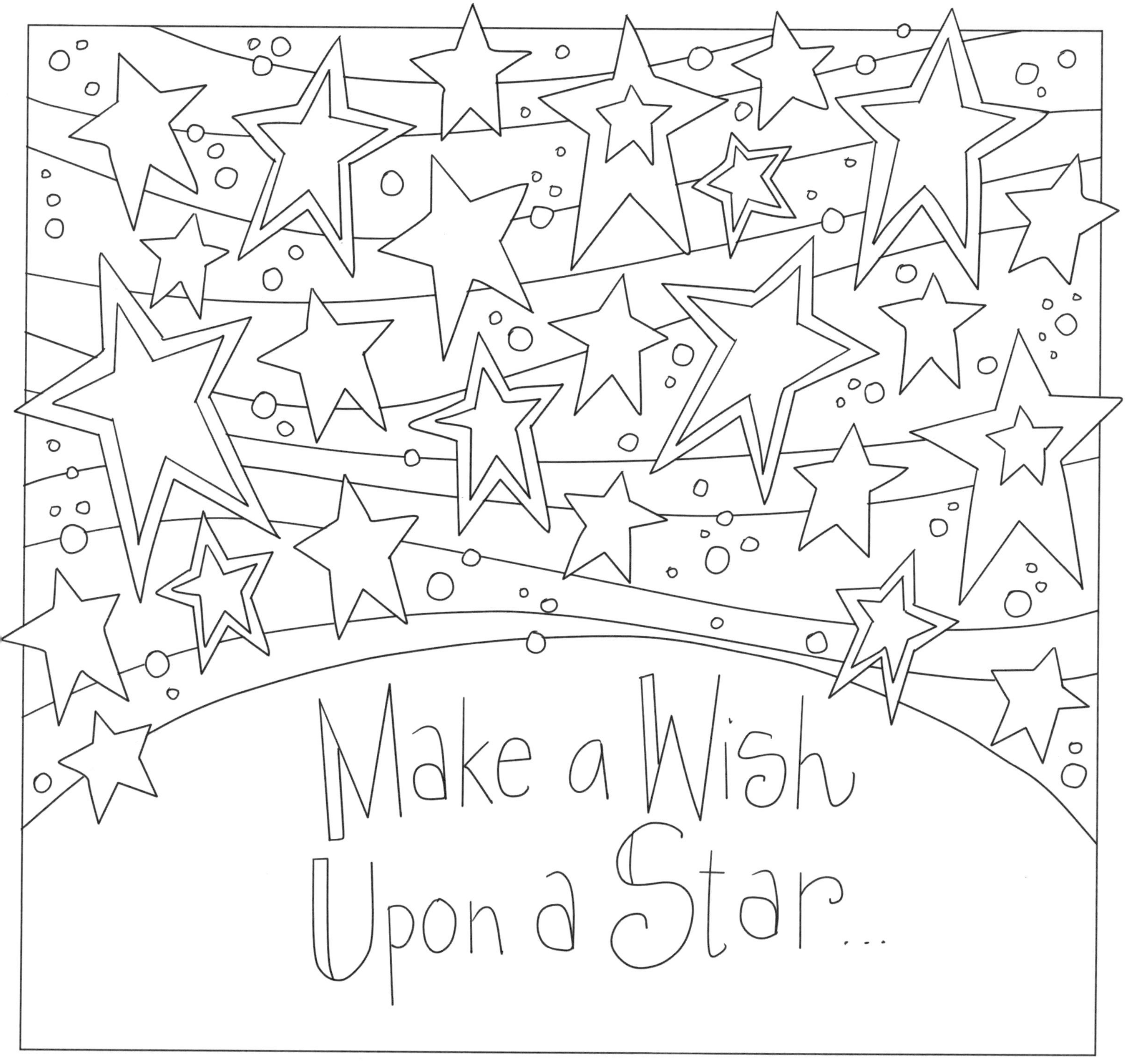
Make a Wish
Upon a Star...

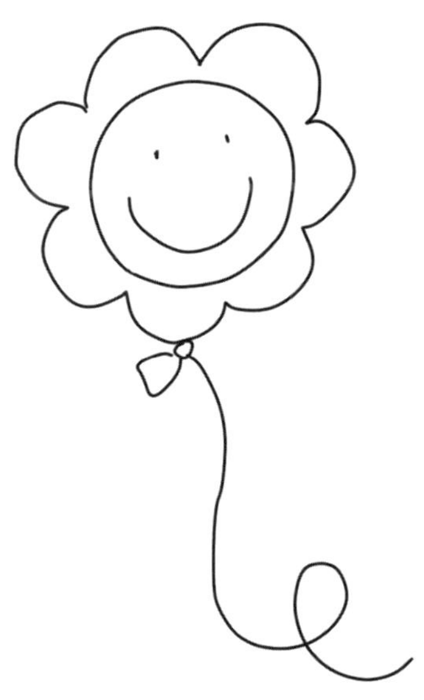

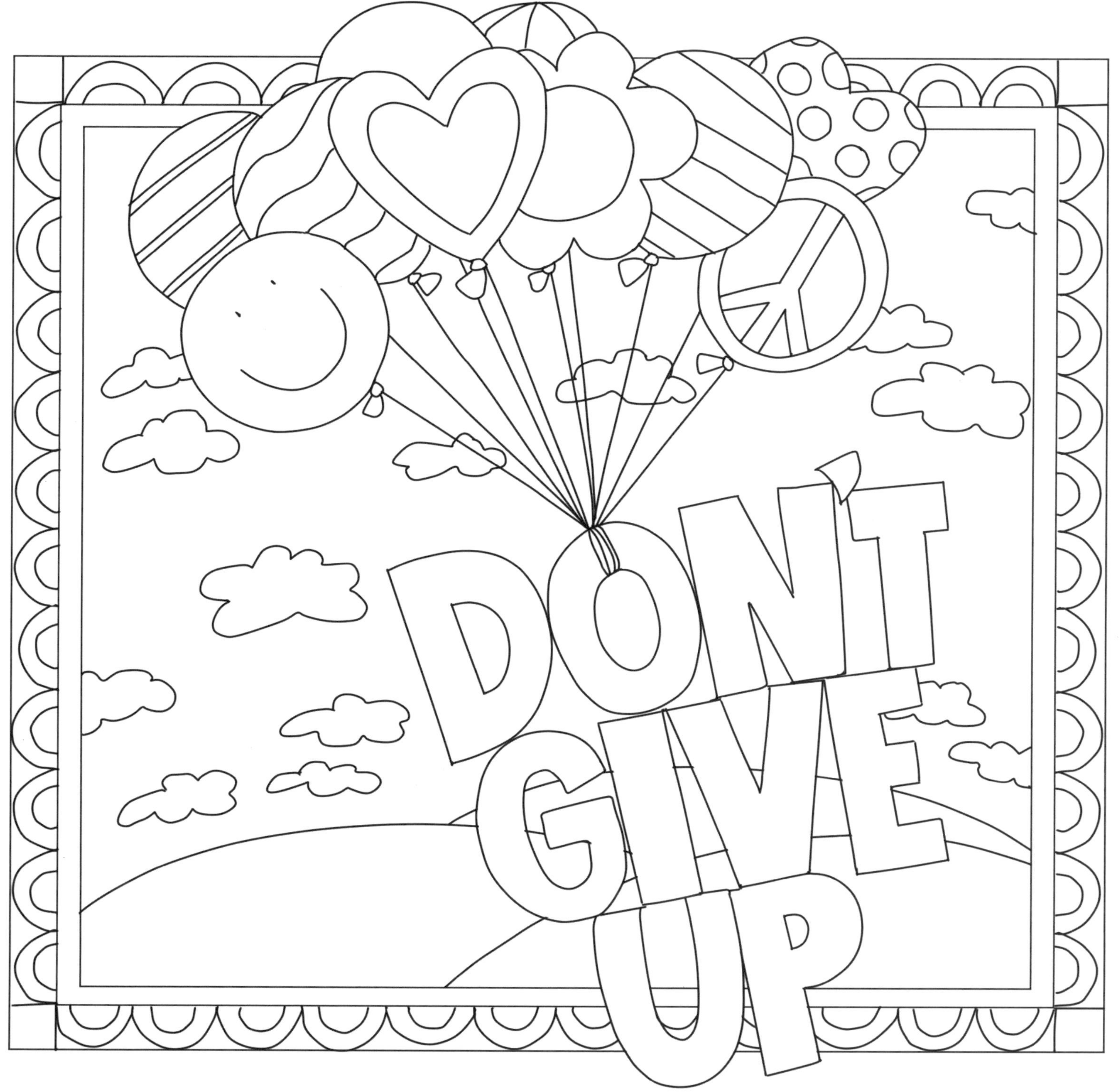
DON'T
GIVE
UP

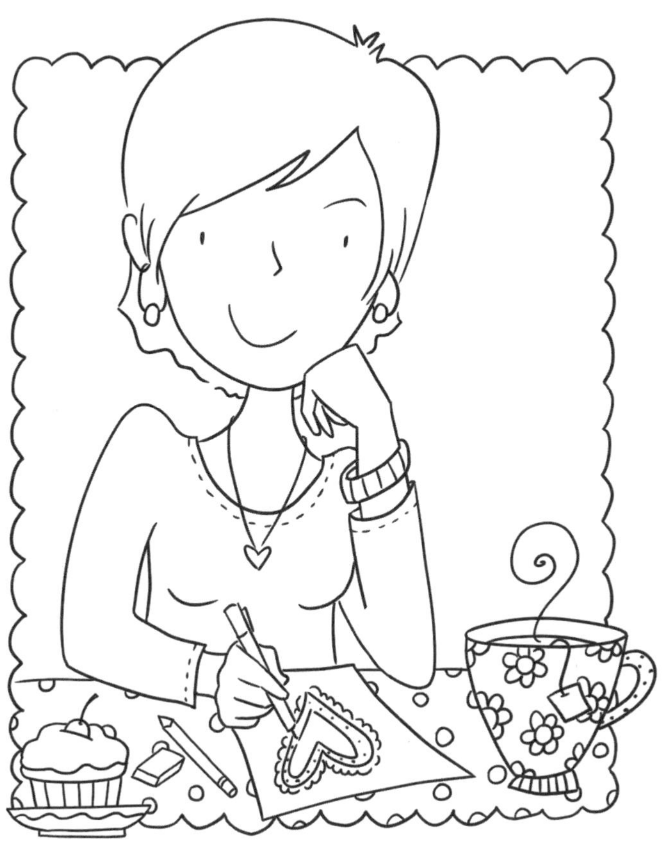

About the Artist

Ronnie Walter has known since she could first hold a crayon what she wanted to do with her life, and that little girl who could draw really well grew up to be a professional artist and author. Her illustrations have been featured on hundreds of products such as stationery and greeting cards, figurines, home and garden products, fabric and much more. She is especially proud of her work creating the Coloring Café® series of coloring books, and of the joy they have brought to thousands of her "Coloristas."

Ronnie lives in paradise with her husband Jim and their colorful Catahoula hound, Larry.

www.thecoloringcafe.com

coloringcafe@gmail.com

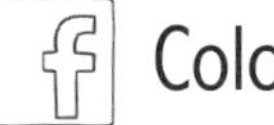 Coloring Café

 The Coloring Café

 @thecoloringcafe

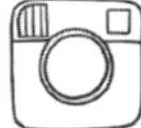 @thecoloringcafe

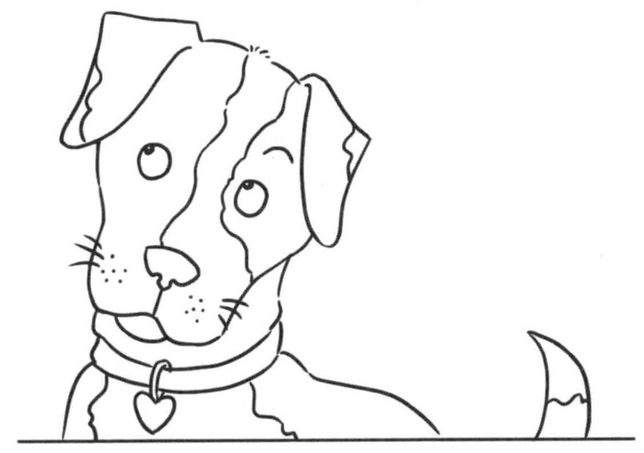

BE STILL MY SOUL

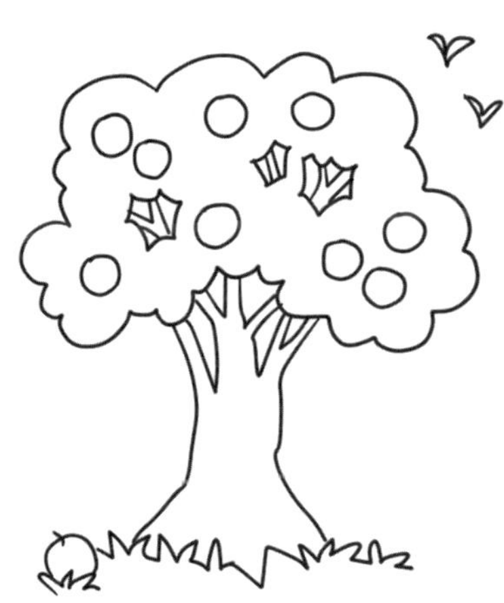

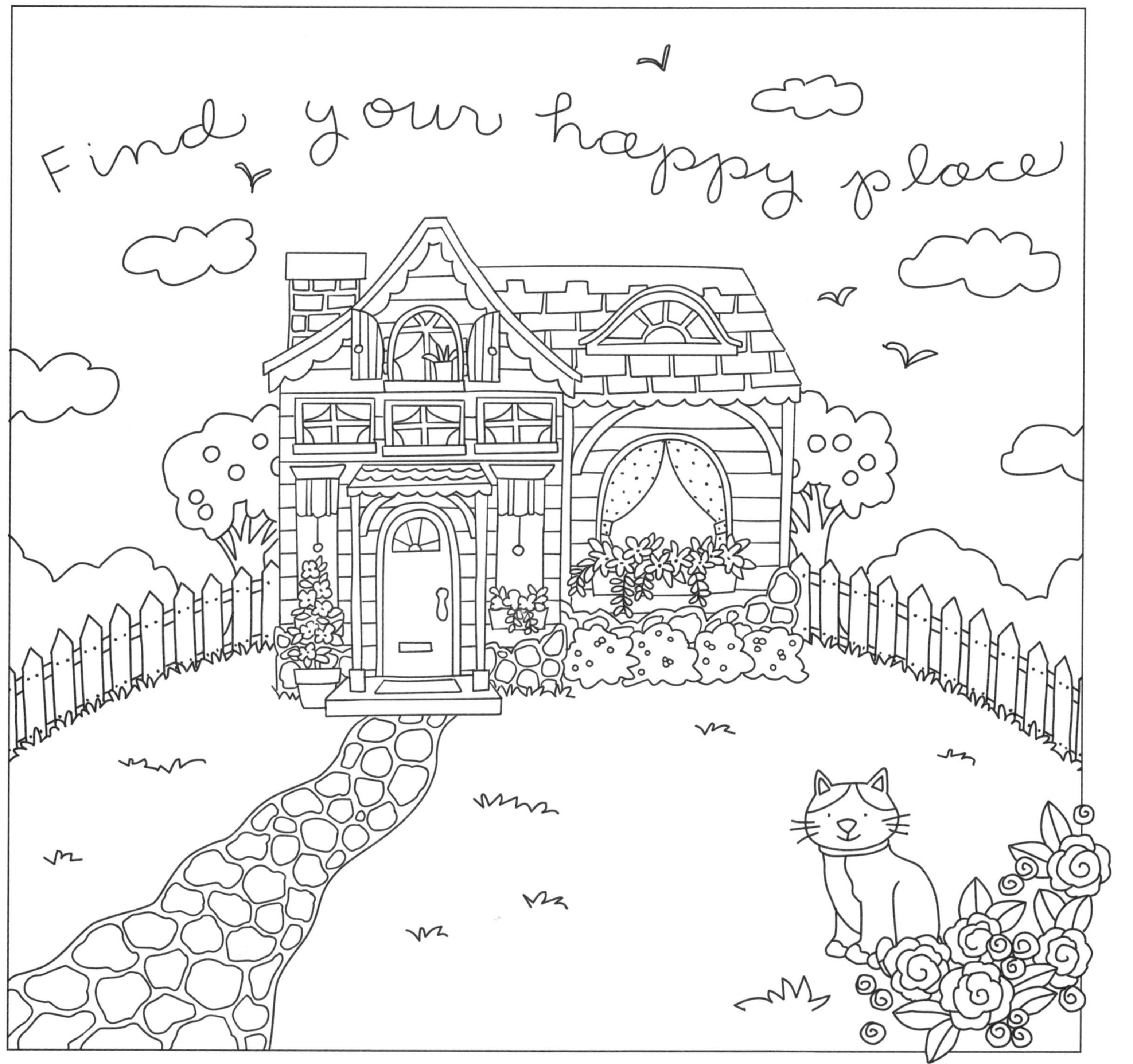
Find your happy place

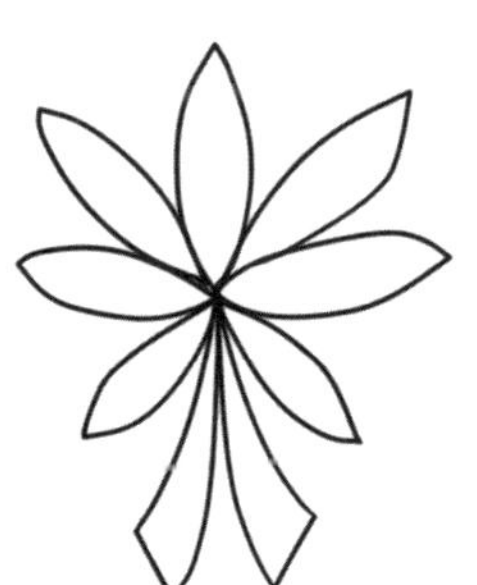

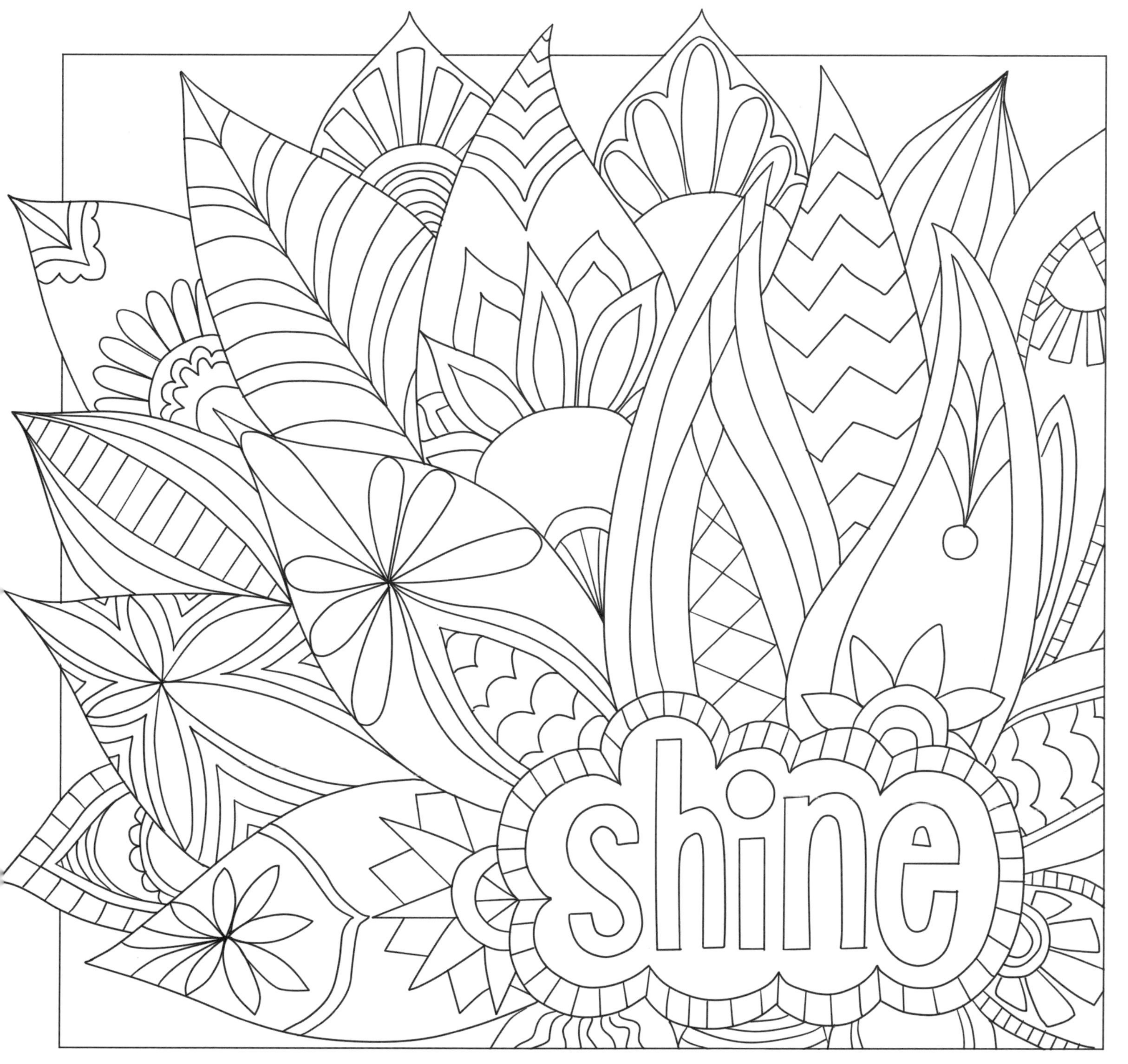
shine

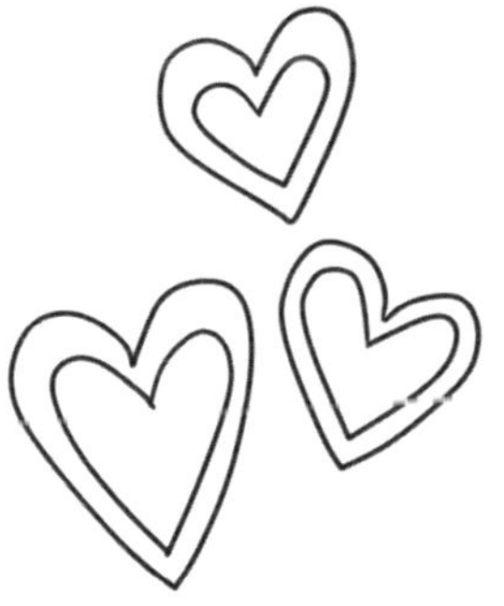

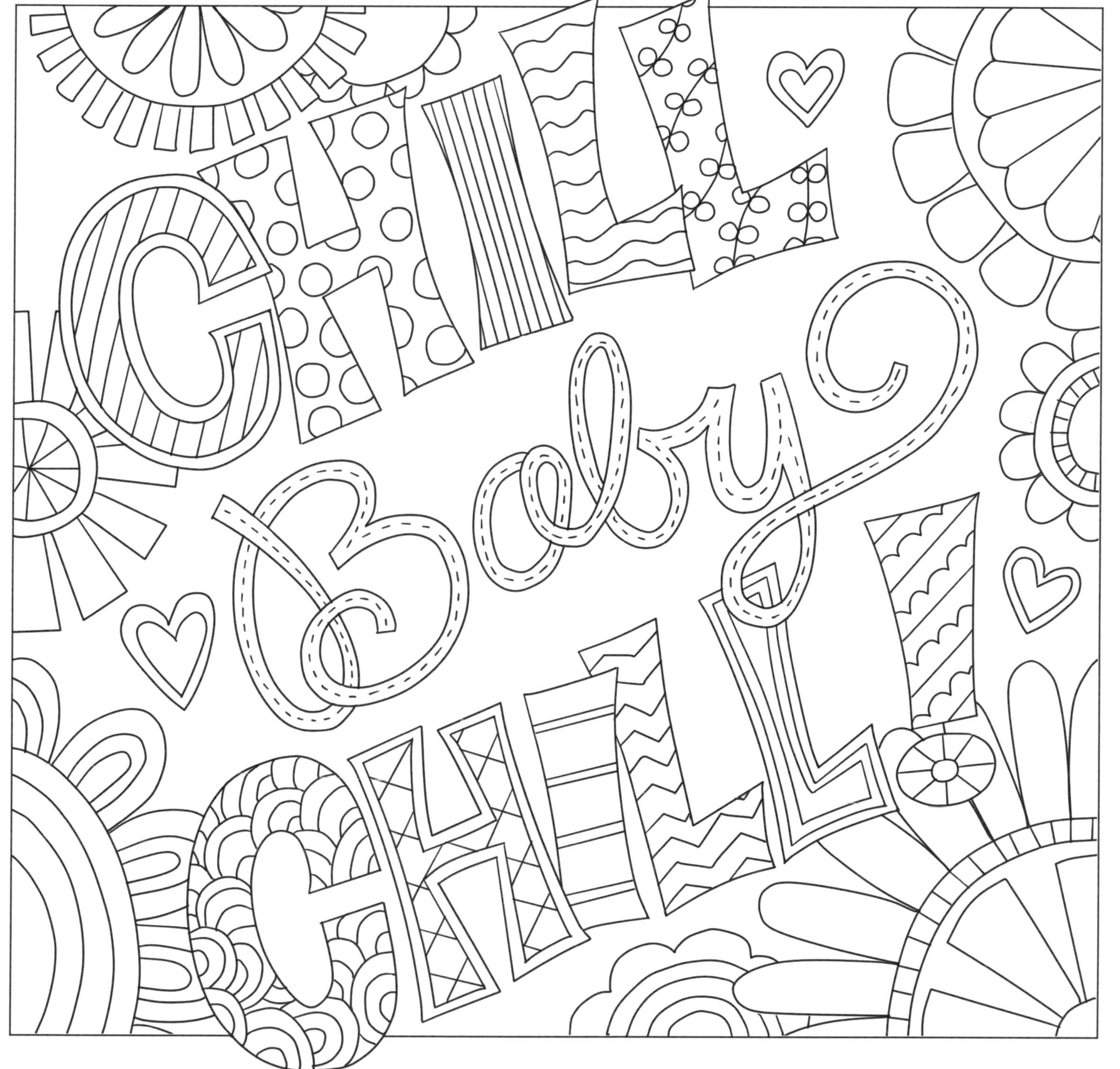
Chill
Baby
Chill!

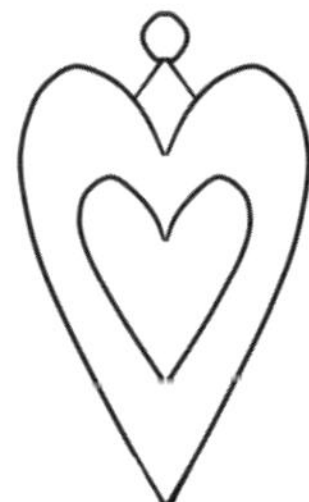

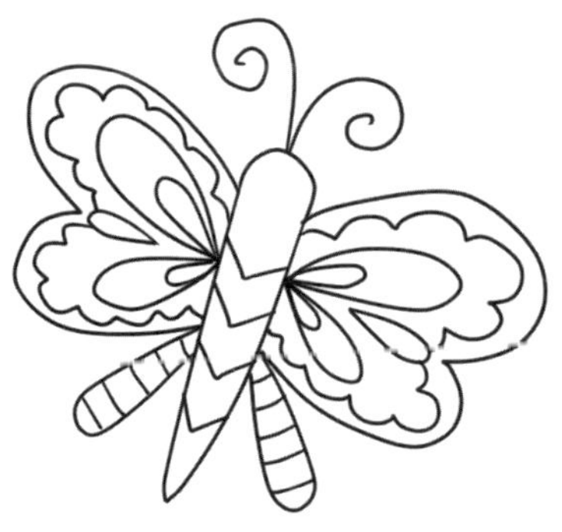

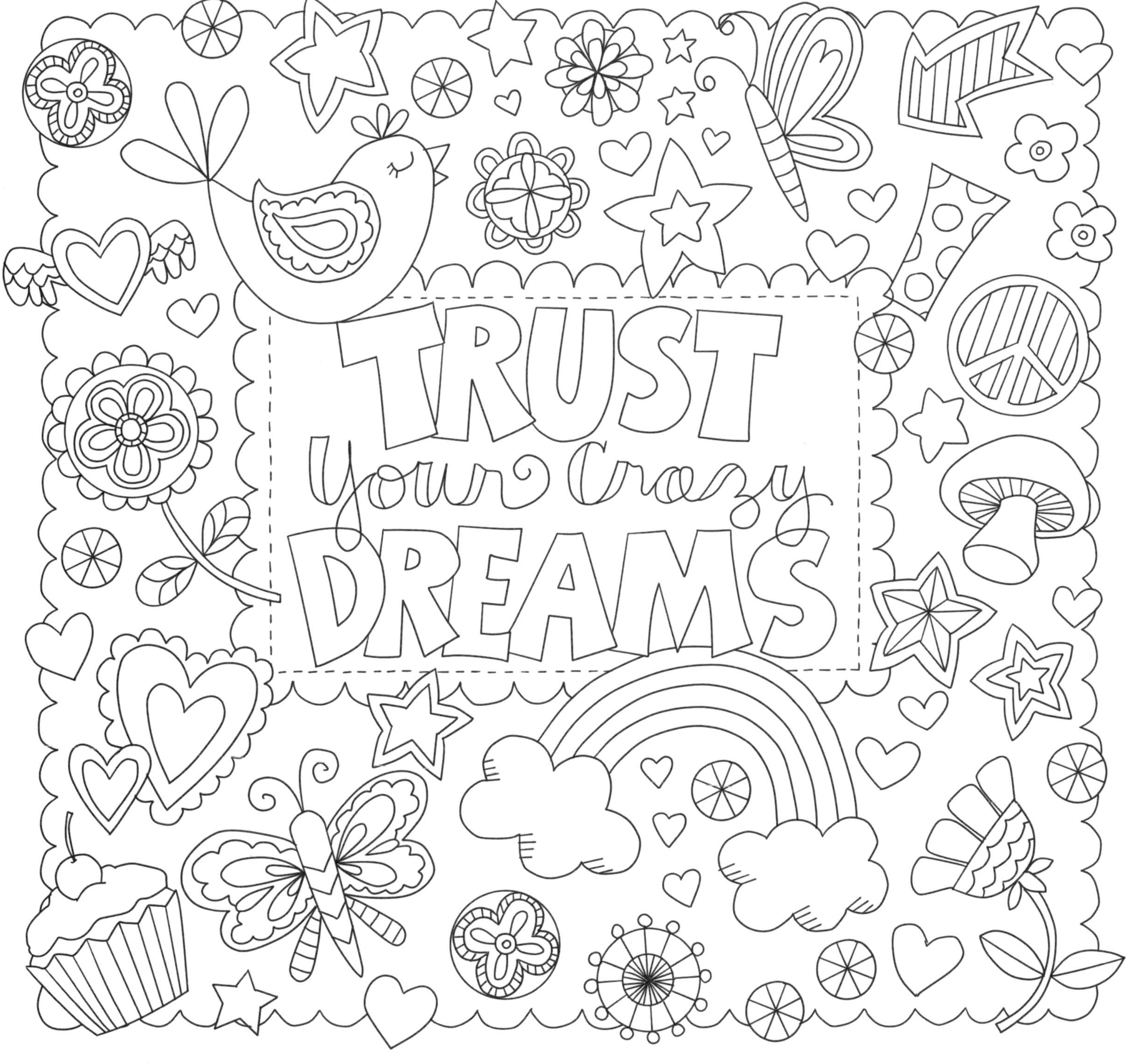
TRUST
Your Crazy
DREAMS

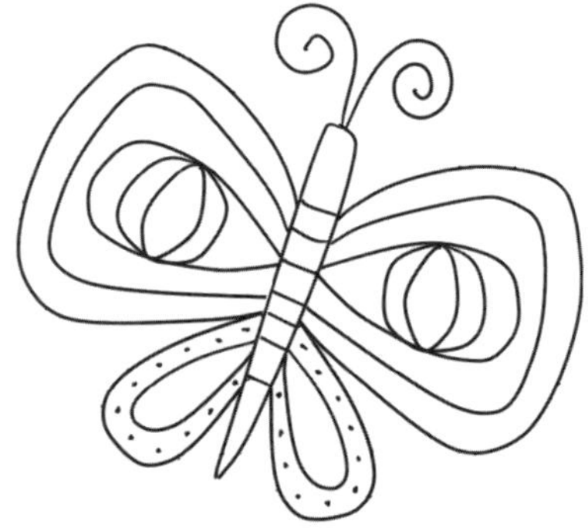

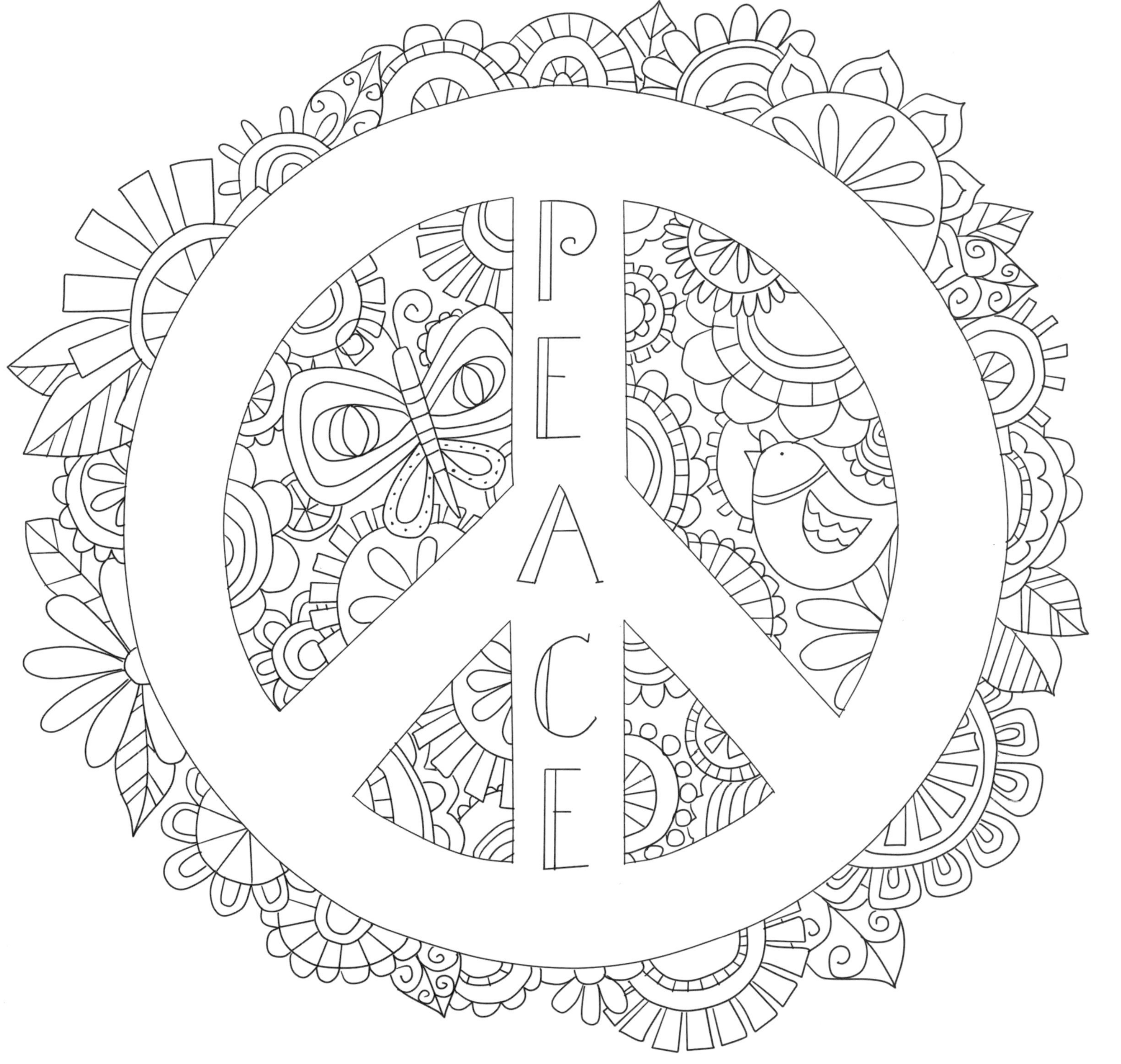
PEACE

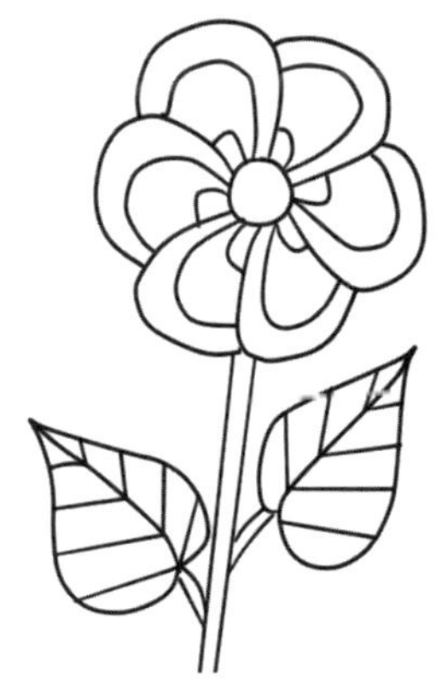

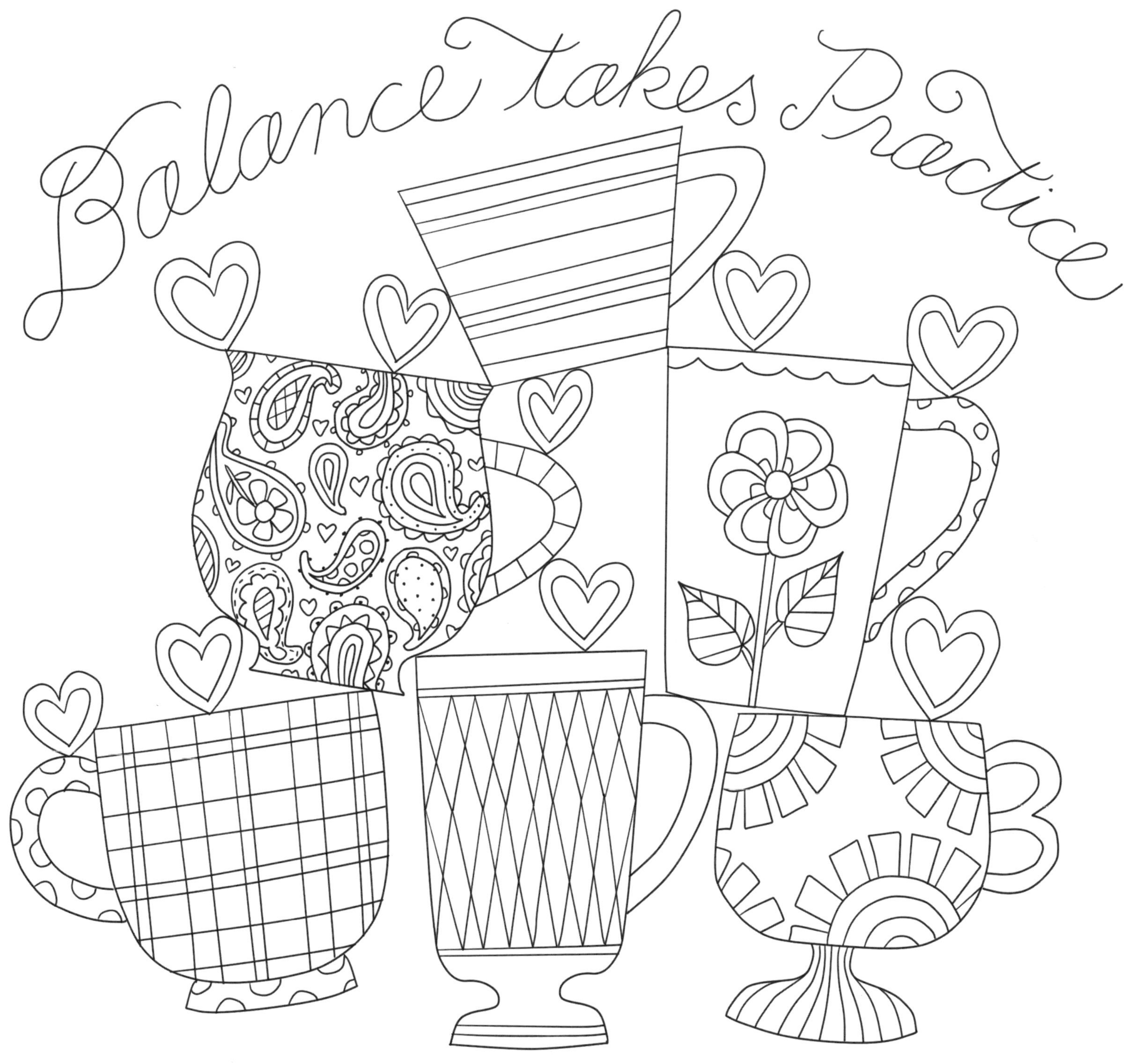
Balance Takes Practice

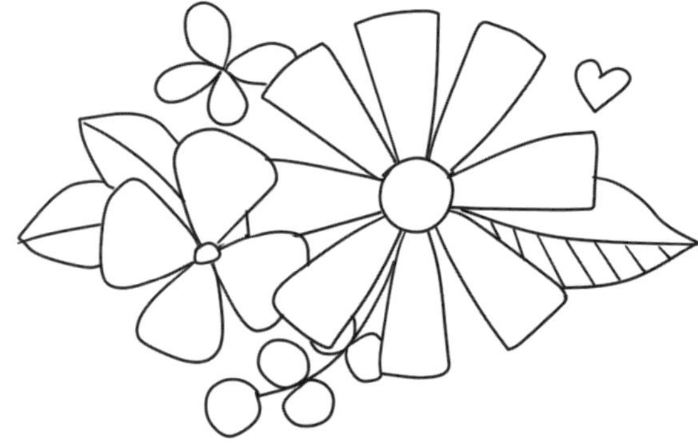

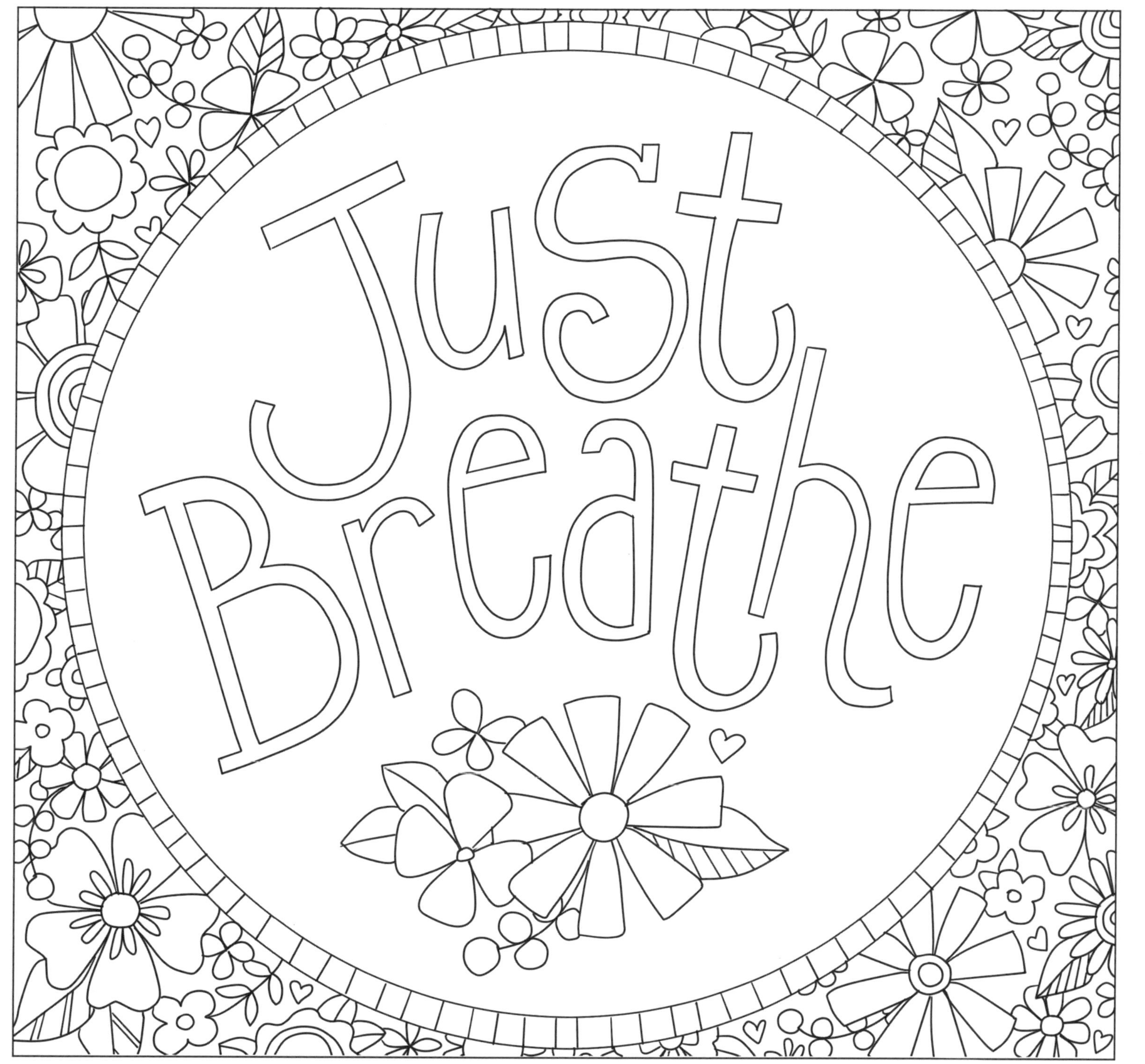
Just Breathe

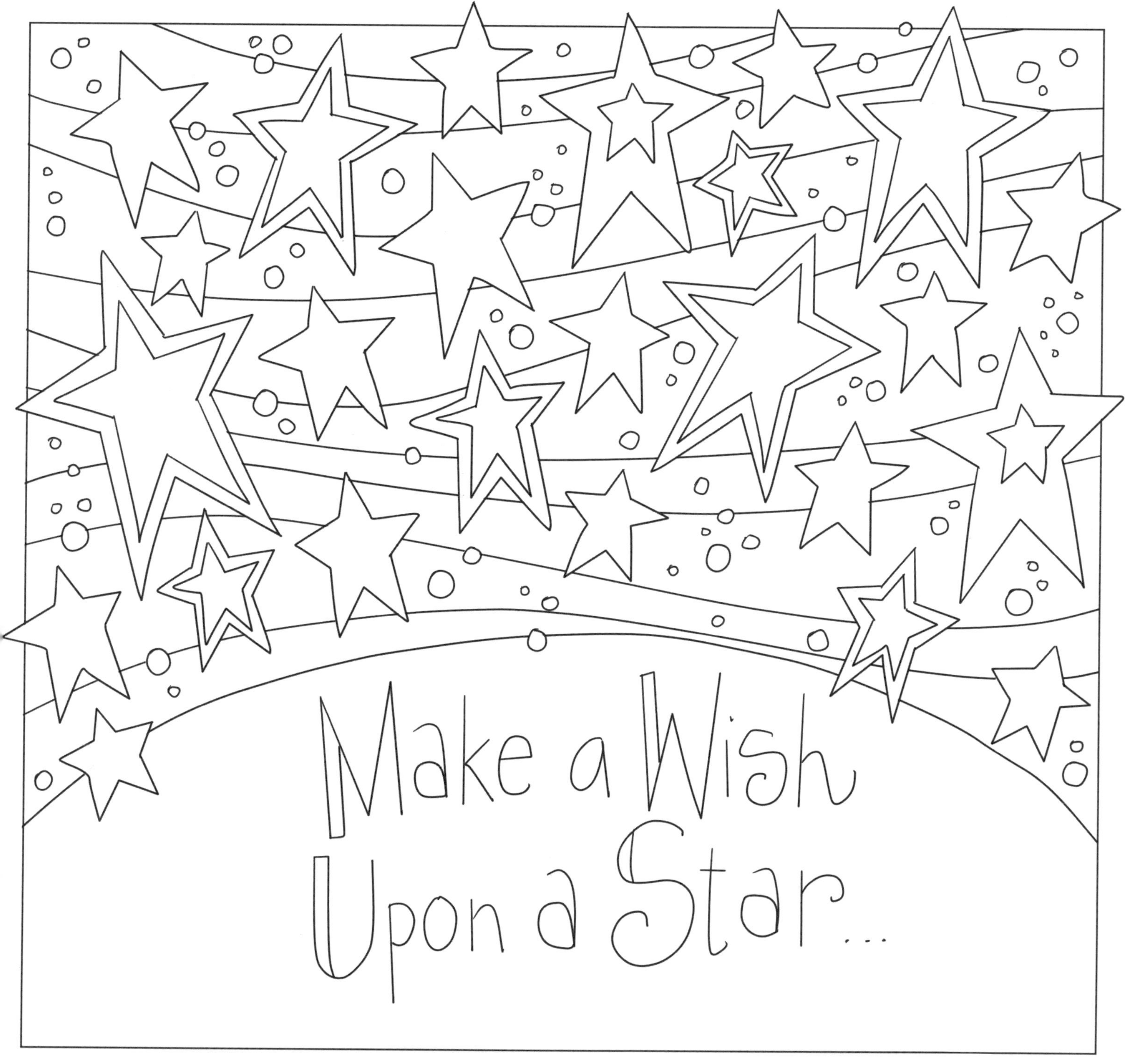
Make a Wish
Upon a Star...

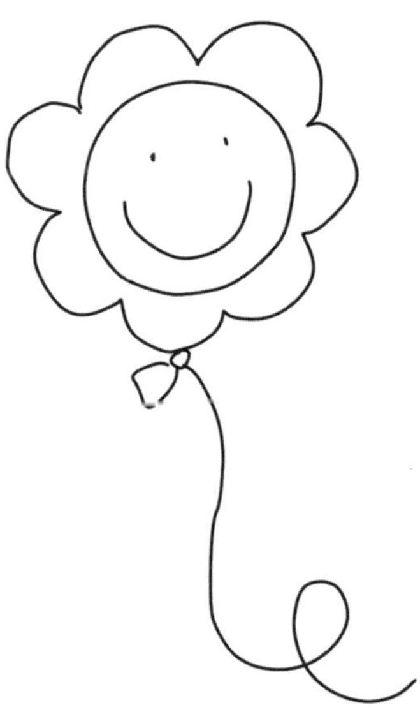

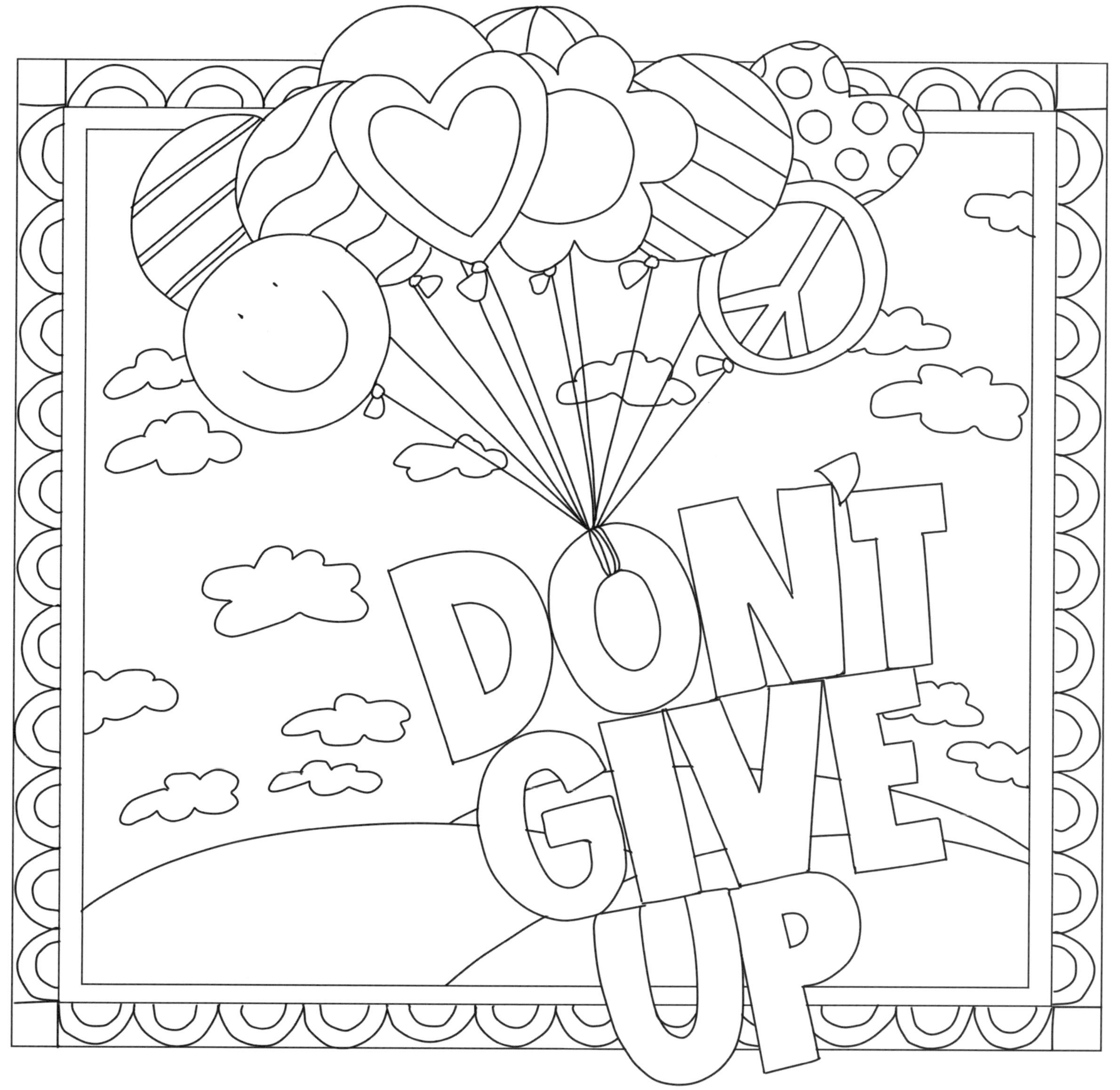
DON'T
GIVE
UP

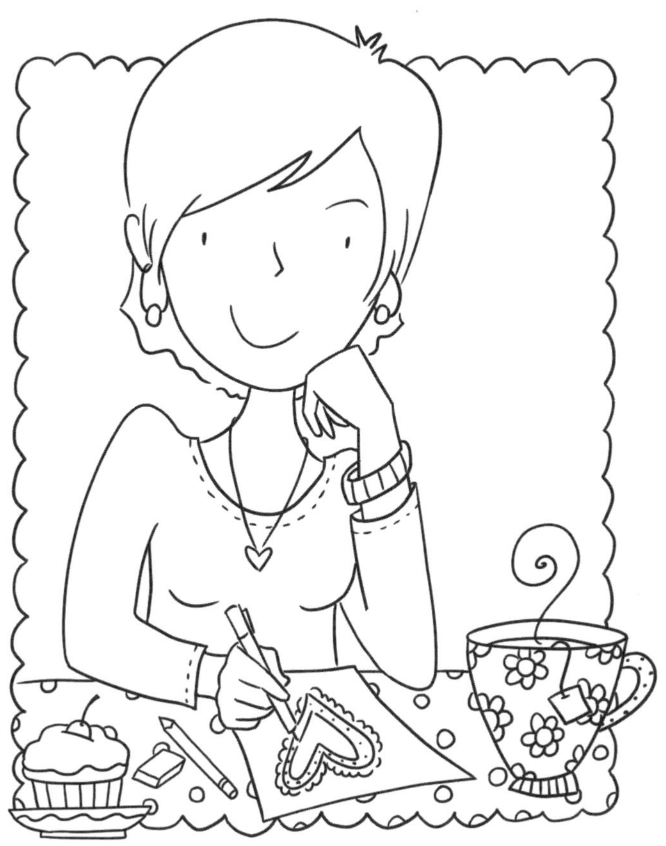

About the Artist

Ronnie Walter has known since she could first hold a crayon what she wanted to do with her life, and that little girl who could draw really well grew up to be a professional artist and author. Her illustrations have been featured on hundreds of products such as stationery and greeting cards, figurines, home and garden products, fabric and much more. She is especially proud of her work creating the Coloring Café® series of coloring books, and of the joy they have brought to thousands of her "Coloristas."

Ronnie lives in paradise with her husband Jim and their colorful Catahoula hound, Larry.

www.thecoloringcafe.com

coloringcafe@gmail.com

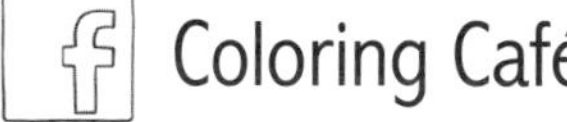
Coloring Café

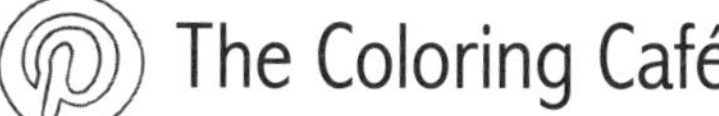
The Coloring Café

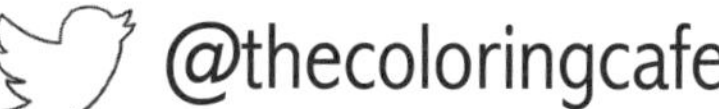
@thecoloringcafe

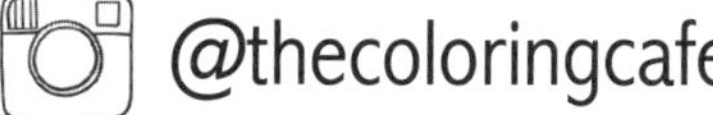
@thecoloringcafe

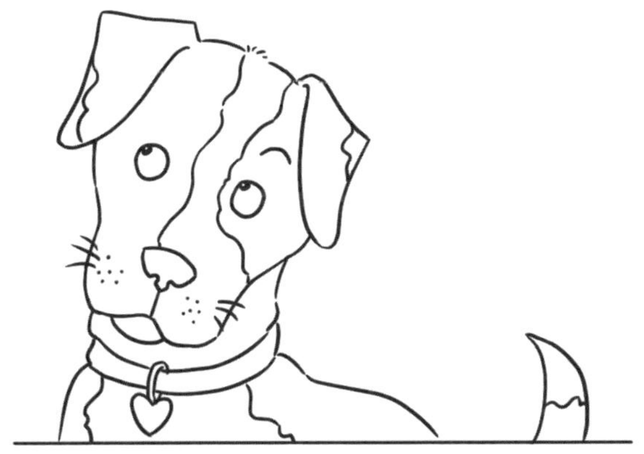

Complete your collection...

with all the coloring products for grown-up girls by The Coloring Café.

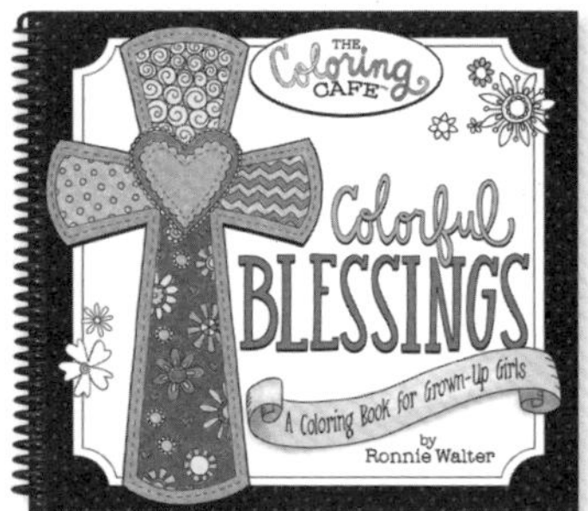

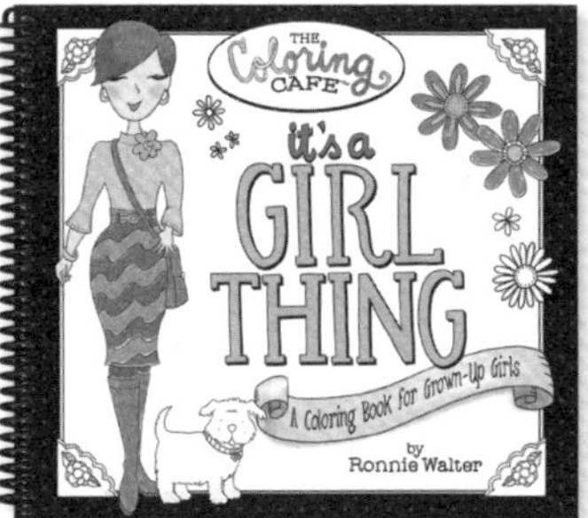

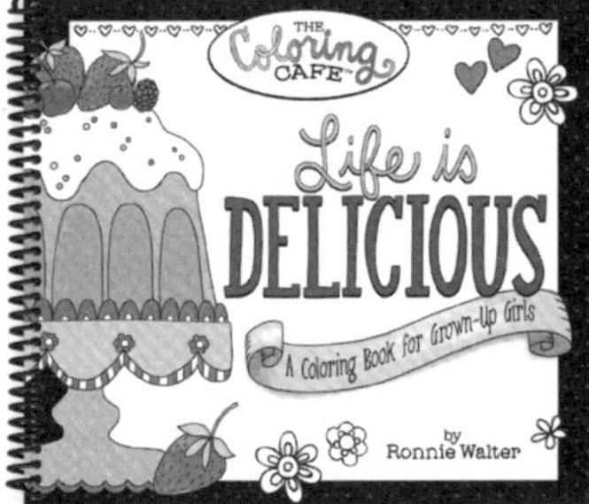

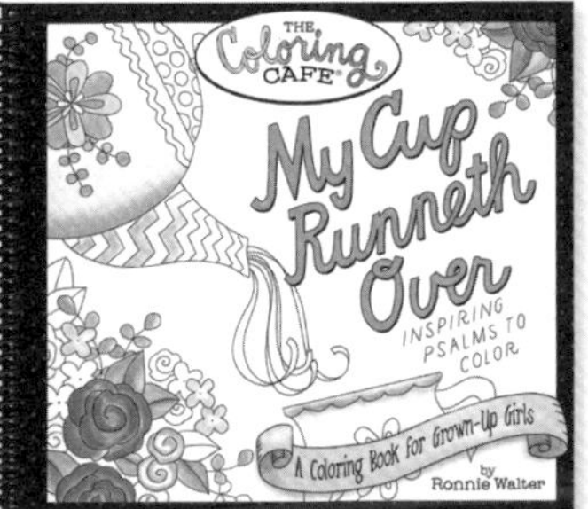

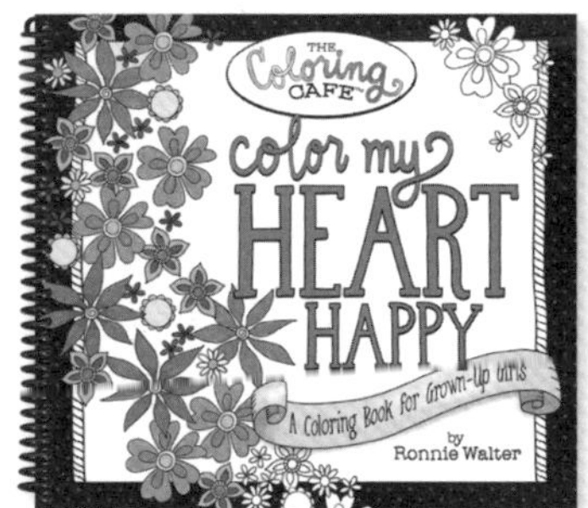

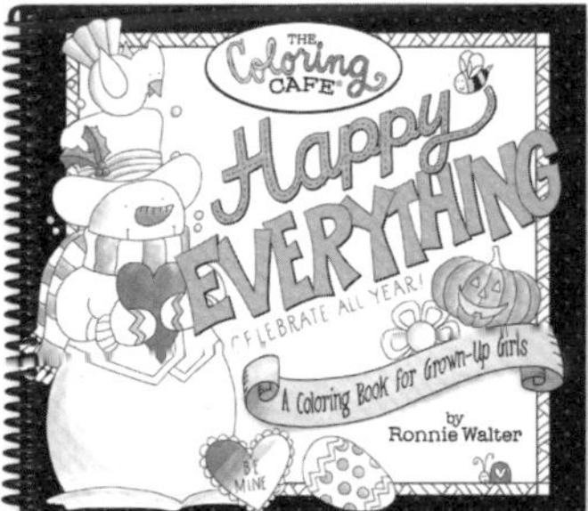

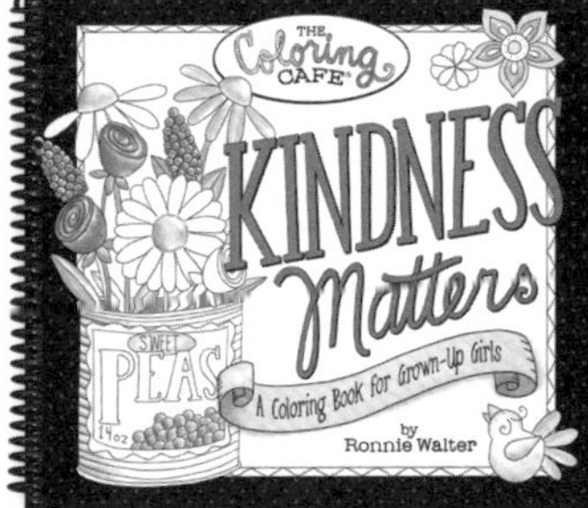

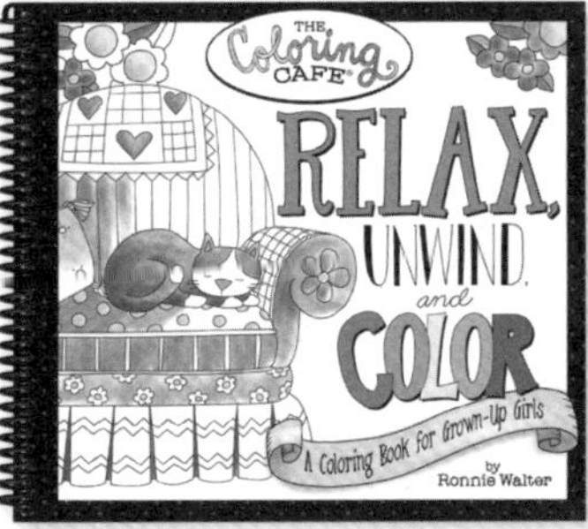

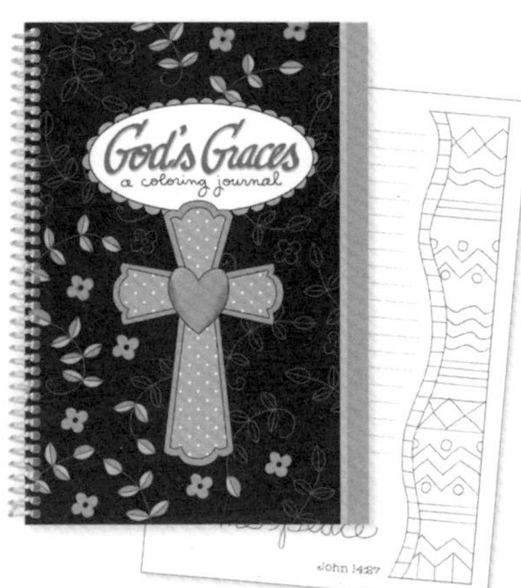

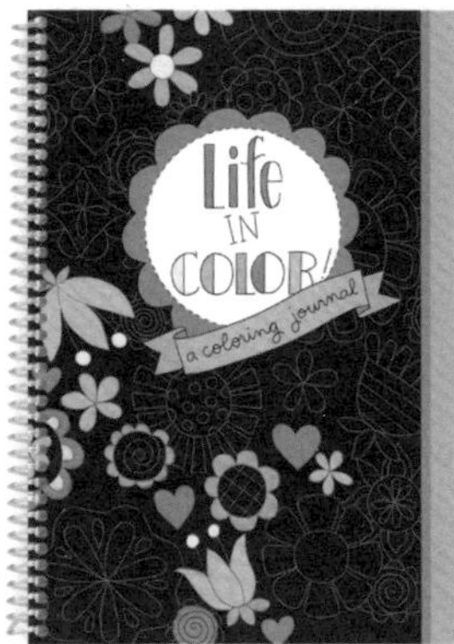

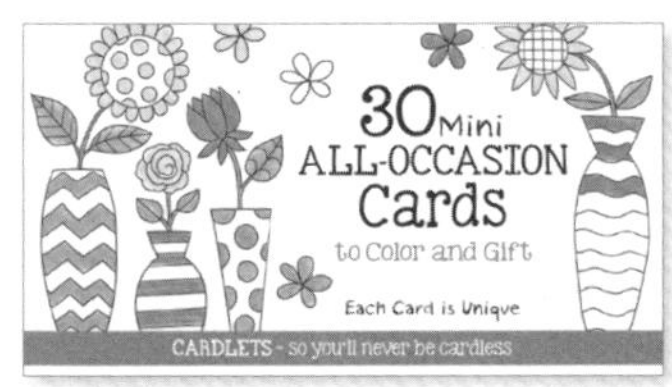

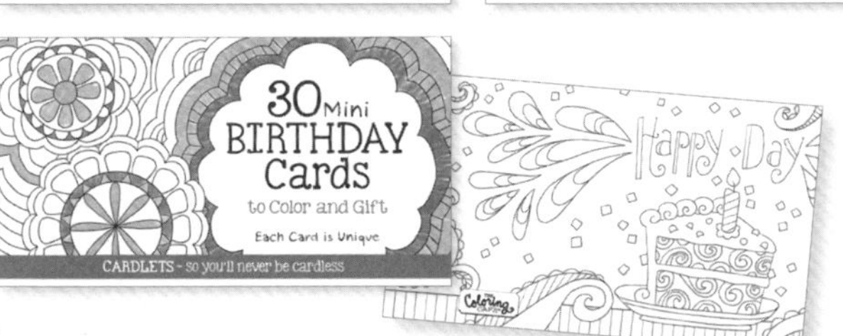

www.cqbookstore.com